Outback Christmas

National Library of Australia Cataloguing-in-Publication entry

Creator:	Habel, Norman, author.
Title:	Outback Christmas / Norman Habel
ISBN:	978-1-925309-48-5 (paperback)
	978-1-925309-49-2 (hardback)
	978-1-925309-50-8 (epub)
	978-1-925309-51-5 (kindle)
	978-1-925309-52-2 (pdf)

ATF PRESS

Making a lasting imprint
An imprint of the ATF Ltd
PO Box 504 Hindmarsh
SA 5007
ABN 90 116 359 963
www.atfpress.com

Graphic Design & Layout: Lydia Paton
Font (Body text): Garamond (12pt)

Outback Christmas

Text by Norman Habel
&
Paintings by Pro Hart

ATF Press
2016

Preface to the 1981 edition

In cultures around the world, the Gospel story has been told in images of word, art, and song which reflect those cultures. In paintings from Japan, Jesus wears typical Japanese clothes and acts in accord with Japanese custom. Crucifixion scenes from Nigeria portray the performers as African. In Papua New Guinea Christmas cards depict the holy family as Papuans.

Most portrayals of the nativity of Christ familiar to Australians are inherited from England or Europe. The holy family regularly appears as Western European rather than Jewish. The Christian teaching that Jesus Christ is the Redeemer of all people's, wherever they are, has lead to the practice of relating the Gospel story to the local context to make it meaningful. Thus the figures of that story are depicted in the language, attire, form, surroundings, and colour of that context. For Christians, the doctrine of the incarnation means that God become a human being for the redemption of all human beings. While we know this event happened in Palestine, it can be interpreted in faith by different peoples as a reality within their own environment. In Jesus Christ, God identified with all humanity, not one particular race.

The paintings of Pro Hart are consistent with this Christian heritage. They portray the nativity of Jesus Christ in bold images of the Australian Outback. Instead of an English Christmas, we here reflect on an Australian bush nativity and its meaning in this context. The incarnation is interpreted as a reality for Australians to explore in terms of their own traditions.

The poems and songs of Norman Habel reflect the same perspective. They interact with the paintings of Pro Hart and seek to complement his work. They draw on images and ideas from the Australian context, especially the poets and artists of the last century. As a portrait of the nativity of Jesus Christ, however, the central themes from the Christian Scriptures dominate the story line.

The ideas and images of this book reflect the search of many Australians to make Christianity in Australia an Australian Christianity. From the traditional Australian carol to recent expressions in art and song, Australians have sought to express their faith in language consistent with the Australian experience. Those who follow are invited to reshape the ideas and make them even more genuinely Australian.

In the last analysis these paintings and poems also reflect the Australian background of their authors: Pro Hart as a lover of the Outback beyond Broken Hill, and Norman Habel from Western Victoria where bushfires could rage at Christmas time.

Norman Habel & Pro Hart

Preface to the 2016 edition

I wrote the poems in *Outback Christmas* almost forty years ago, exploring the cultural relevance of the story of Jesus' birth as written in the Gospels. My partner, Pro Hart, was also exploring how the birth narratives were relevant in the Outback, where he lived.

As I read again what I have written, I discern themes and mysteries expressed in Aussie jargon, that still ring true to me.

The characters of the narrative are not glorified or romanticised as in classical medieval art but portrayed as down-to-Earth figures from the Outback. Joseph is just an 'ordinary bloke', Zechariah is a 'rough bush priest', and Mary is a 'quiet country girl', who knew tales of bunyips and devil dogs.

The incarnation is not depicted as a spectacular wonder, but a pregnancy and birth that reflects the rough life of a woman in the Outback, a woman forced to give birth in a stable behind a pub, where stockmen drink through the night and tell loud bawdy tales. As Mary says, 'in the silence of the dawn, Jesus bursts from my body gasping for life and shedding his robe of blood'.

A theme that still resonates with me is the portrayal of 'God as the Silence of the Outback, the Silence beyond the black of the sweeping night sky, the Silence of the timeless Rock at the hot centre'. Mary declares the 'Silence is broken when my son was born and God became a parent.'

Anna's Song was sung far and wide as a celebration of the birth of Jesus, a song that reflects a series of rites from around the world that are performed when a child is born. For example, verse 2 reflects the custom of laying the child on the ground to bond with Mother Earth:

> *Human clay, human birth.*
> *Lay this child on the ground,*
> *Let God know in his Son,*
> *One with us, one with Earth.*

The significance of Jesus' birth, in the context of this reading of the birth narrative, is reflected in the final verse:

Lift this child to the night,
To the Silence of God,
Let this child cry for us
And the Silence be heard.

Music was written for this song and other poems in the volume by Robin Mann, when we performed *Outback Christmas* as a stage production. For several years *Outback Christmas* was performed in churches, schools and local communities. Robin Mann also made a CD that was true to the spirit of the poems and paintings.

By reprinting *Outback Christmas*, I wish to honour Pro Hart for the extraordinary way in which he captured the spirit of the Outback and the story of Jesus' birth in that context. One quote that he frequently made in response to the 'Silence of God' in the poetry of the book is, 'Norm, God is Now! Now!' Thanks Pro for your friendship, your generosity, your images and your Outback spirit. May your spirit live on in this reprint.

Norman Habel

Contents

Preface to the 1981 edition	*4*
Preface to the 2016 edition	*6*
Contents	*9*
The Coming Bushman	*10*
Zechariah's Vision	*12*
Zechariah's Silence	*14*
Old Joseph the Carpenter	*16*
Mary's Fear	*18*
The Joy of Elizabeth	*20*
Zechariah's Pride	*22*
The Ride to Bethlehem	*24*
The Bethlehem Pub	*26*
Jesus's Birth	*28*
The Stockmen's Story	*30*
Report of the Stockmen	*32*
Mary's Gift	*34*
Simeon's Farewell	*36*
Anna's Song	*38*
The Three Gamblers	*40*
Gold Rush	*42*
Herod's Apology	*44*
The Gifts of the Gamblers	*46*
The Flight	*48*
Coming Home	*50*
About the Author	*52*
About the Illustrator	*53*

The Coming Bushman

Ours is a story of Christmas
out back
when Jesus the Bushman was born,
a story of Mary
and Joseph and Jesus,
good folk like us from the bush.

We are the gamblers, the stockmen,
the wise,
the women who battle the scrub,
the people who wear
no airs on their face
and know the price of a grave.

Years we have waited for someone
to come
born out of true country stock,
a bushman foretold
by drovers of old,
a battler as straight as a die.

Late 'round the campfire we sang
of our dream,
a man who is one with the bush,
a man who would gamble
his life for his friends
and know the silence of God.

Ours is a story of Jesus
the Bushman,
born behind Bethlehem's pub,
a boy who was born
to be king of the bush
and dies for his mates in the end.

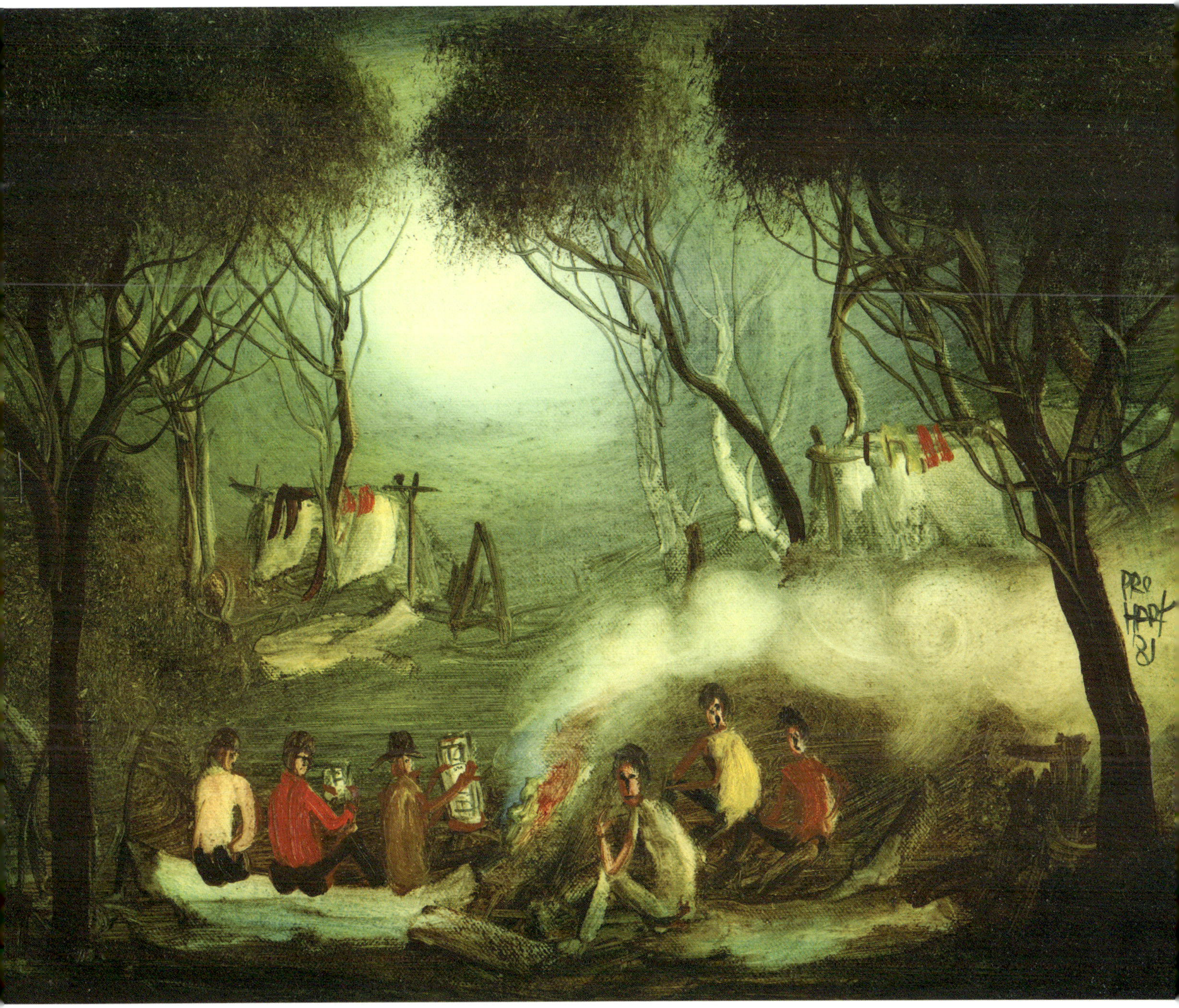

Zechariah's Vision

I am Zechariah,
a rough bush priest.
People trust me for what I am,
the voice of their God
echoing through the hard times.

Their God is
the Silence of the Outback,
the Silenceof the Dreaming
alive in the landscape,
the Silence beyond the black
of the sweeping night sky,
the Silence within the dry soil
that opens to the seed
when the bushfire roars overhead,
the Silence of the timeless rock
at the hot centre,
the Silence after the grinding
blinding dust storm,
the Silence before the brown rain
crashes into the dust the blood
to end the drought,
the Silence of the Outback.

He is silent, but there,
out back,
there, as bush folk work the scrub,
there, as they battle the land,
and grit their teeth on the dust.
I am his voice,
his weak speech in the night.

One day he broke the silence
and sent an angel,
his own bush angel.
It stood beside the altar
a slim brown figure,
a bird engulfed in flame.

'Don't be scared', the angel said,
'Your wife will have a son
and you will call him John.
He'll be filled with the Spirit of God,
wild as Elijah, a bushman,
a prophet of the wilderness
calling people to God . . .
and more than that,
he'll never touch wine
or drink a beer like other men.'

I stood alone
. . . speechless.

Luke 1:8–20

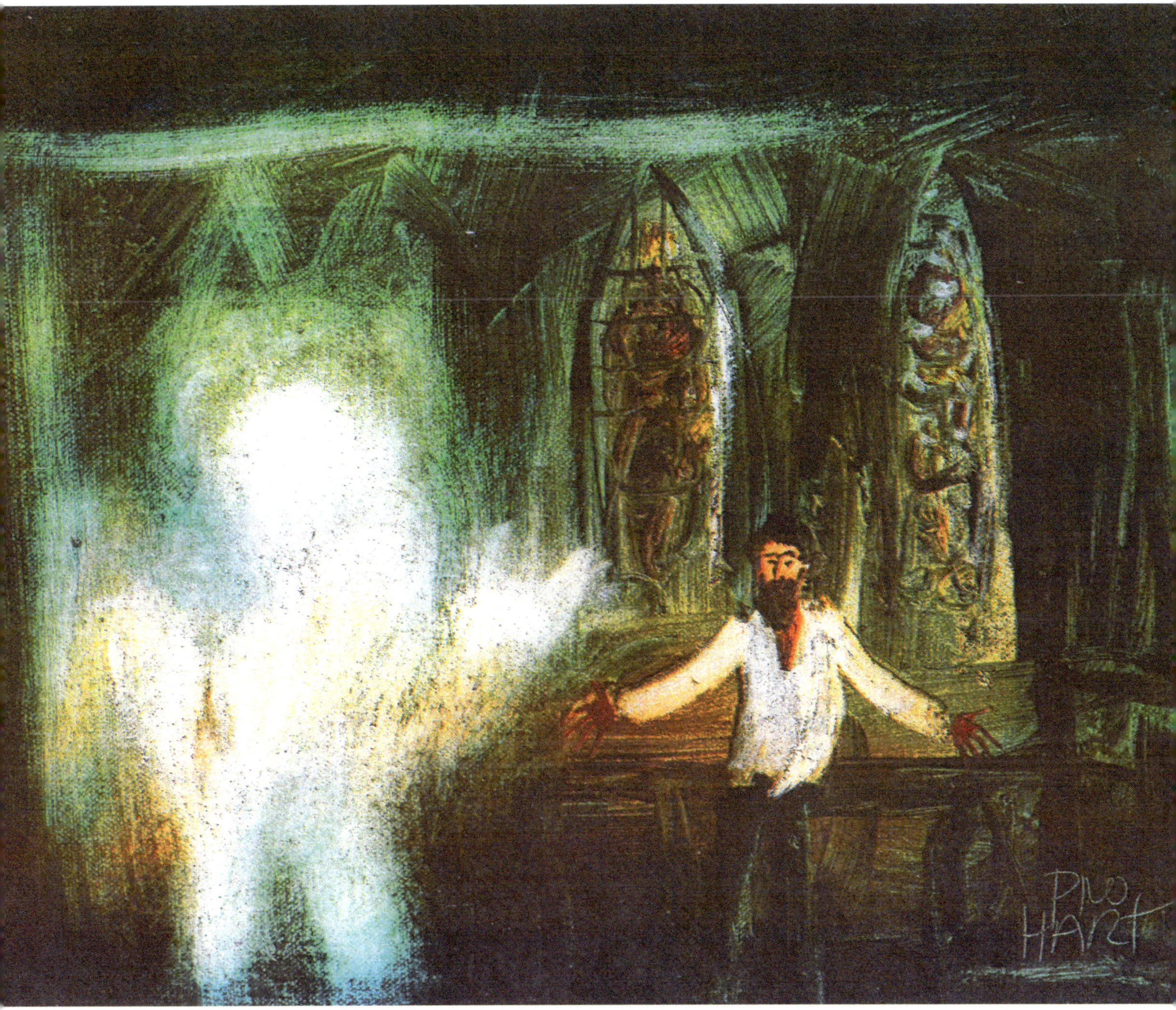

Zechariah's Silence

After the bush angel left
I was speechless,
Dumb as a mouthless stone.
When I tried to speak to the folks
Waiting in the heat outside,
The silence was cruel.
They could barely hear
The groan of the old rusted windmill,
The crude call of a solitary crow,
or the twisted shuffle
of a sunbaked lizard across the dust.

Nothing moved.

I scratched my signs in the dust
beside the lizard's trail
and the track of a snake now hiding
in the woodwork of God's house.
'I SAW A BUSH ANGEL',
I scrawled,
'NOW I AM DUMB.
GO HOME
WHILE I HAVE MY SON.'

My country fold looked at me
In knowing pain and shock.
'Poor old beggar,
he's off his head
The Bush has got to his brain.
He'll never be like us again.
He preached about the Silence,
The hidden God out back.
Now the old man's speechless too,
Just like his silent God.'

I wandered home through the haze
And held my old wife Liz.
The silence is strong
When old people make love
on a quiet evening
Under dust-filled skies out back

Luke 1:21–23

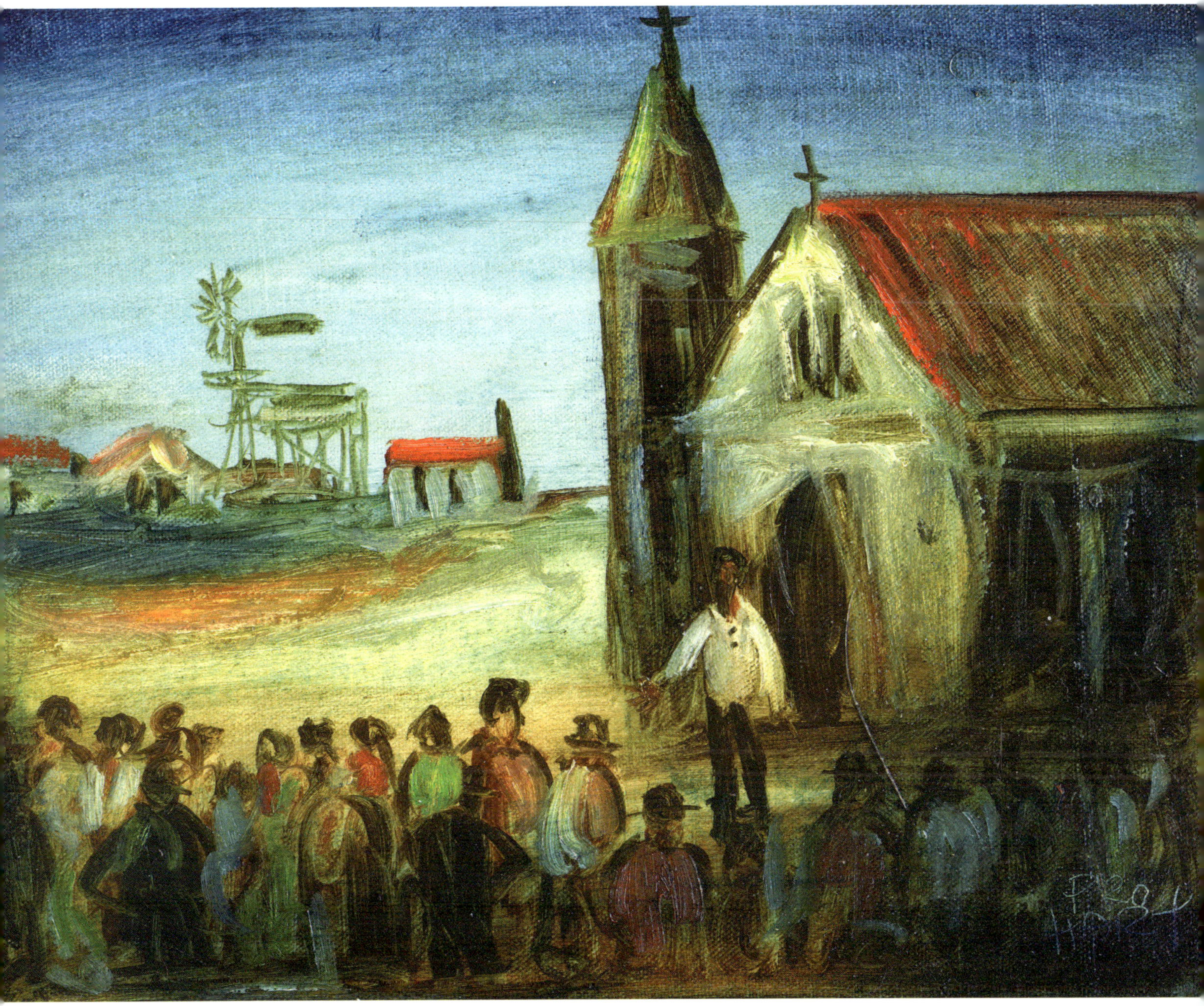

Old Joseph the Carpenter

I was just an ordinary bloke
before the baby came,
and I still am.
I never looked down on any man
though men have laughed at me
for what has happened.
My hands are torn
by the sharp wood and rough tools
of a country carpenter.
But I never looked down on anyone,
especially a girl like Mary.

Mary was a gentle girl
before the baby came,
a slender sapling ready
for the wind to stretch with life.
She would sit on a log nearby
and wonder
as I kept pounding, pounding,
pounding nails into the wounded wood.
She knew the wood was being broken
to yield shelters for weary frames
or feedboxes for hungry animals.

I told her once
that when she grew older
we could perhaps get married.
Then one cruel afternoon
with a hot North wind like fire,
I found her in the family way.
The pain in my chest was burning me
as if a spike had ruptured my lung.
God only knows
how she came by the child.
I swear I never touched her,
not me, not Joseph the carpenter.
But did the right thing by her
and no one can say I didn't.

Then the baby came
and the baby was . . .
beautiful!

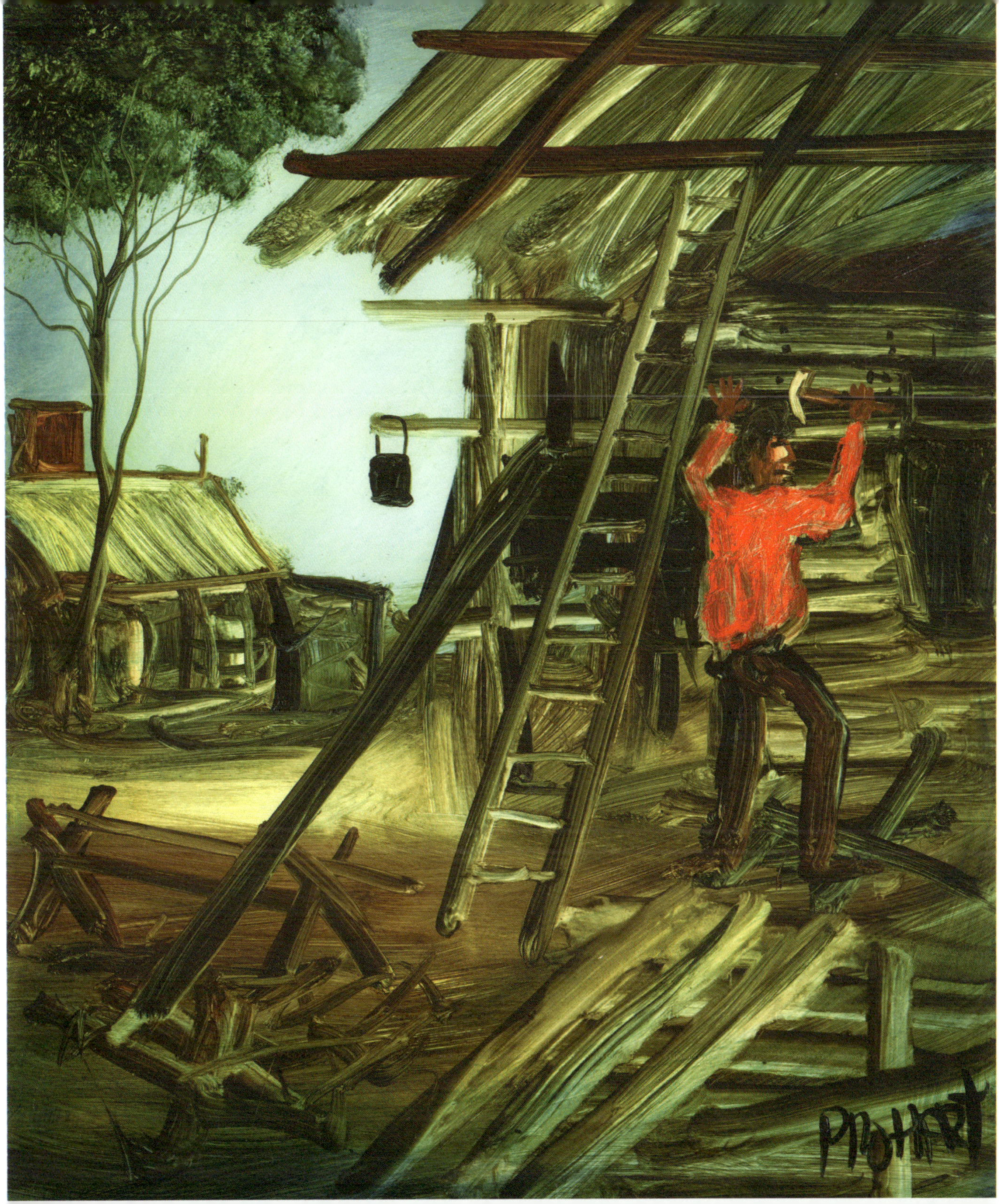
Prophet

Mary's Fear

I am Mary,
a quiet country girl
caught in a web of anxious dreams,
I have heard tall tales
of bunyips, devil dogs, and ghosts
waiting in the bush shadows
to scare the wits from a child.

Yet when the bush angel appeared
it seemed kind,
a slim brown figure
dancing with smiles before me,
like a lyrebird
framed in a silhouette of fire.

'Don't be afraid', the angel said,
'You have been chosen by God
to have a child called Jesus.
He will be God's Son;
Son of the Silent One
high above.'

I quivered in fear
like a lost baby bird.

'How?' I whispered,
'How can I have a child
when I don't even have a husband?'

'A shadow will hover over you
one night', the angel said,
'the Spirit from the Dreaming
will plant a seed within you,
the Spirit of God himself.
In time, you will have his Son.'

The angel's words terrified me.
I clutched my virgin womb
and held it tightly,
afraid of the cold unknown
about to pierce my body.

Luke 1:26–38

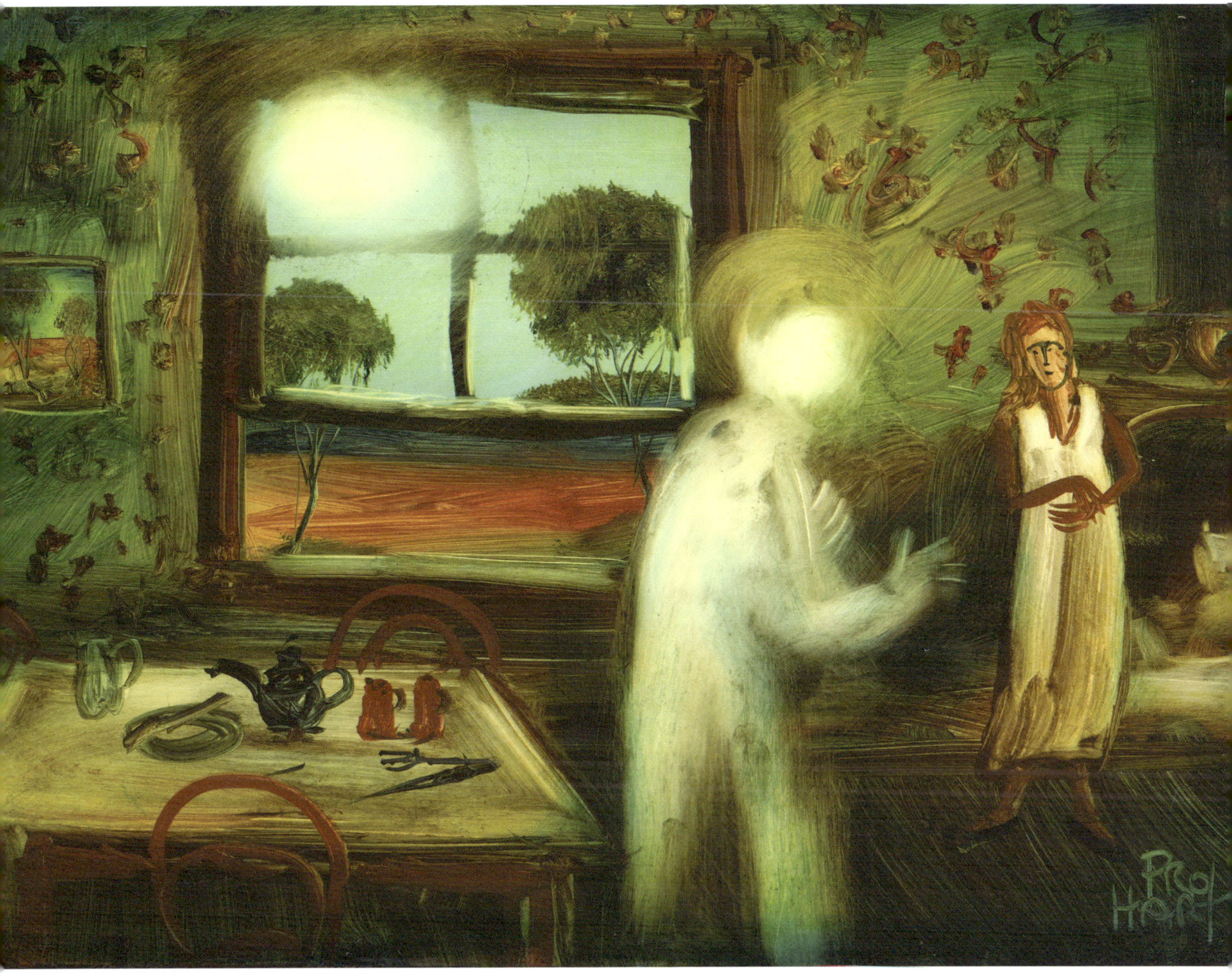
Pro
Hart

The Joy of Elizabeth

I know the bite of death,
the taste of bitter drought,
the task of battling on
and on and on
against the lonely odds of life out back.
I know too the drought within,
a womb refusing to yield up life
and splash these walls with laughter.

I was getting on in years
when my tired womb began to swell
like wet wheat within me.
For six long months I waited,
waited for a sign of life,
the trace of a toe against my bladder,
a flutter beneath my heart.
Nothing!
Nothing but slow swelling.
Was it an ugly growth,
the thick tongue of death?
Was it another sad joke
sent by our cruel-desert God
as if favouring rabbits over humans.
Or was it the wonder child
the angel promised my dumb husband
in one of his blurred visions?

I watched my cousin Mary walk that day
across the bare brown paddocks
snarling beneath a summer haze.

'Liz', she called, 'How are you?
It's really good to are you.'

Her words sent a rush of life
speeding through my body
and deep into my womb.
The baby broke its six-month sleep
and leaped
in bounds of gentle thunder.

Tears flowed down my cheeks
and I could not contain myself.
'Mary! Mary! You are the one.
You have been chosen by God.
Your child will be his Son.'

It was wonderful, that day,
being a woman,
knowing my child was alive,
knowing I was not alone.

In the distance, too, the thunder
spoke of an end to the taste of drought.

Luke 1:39–56

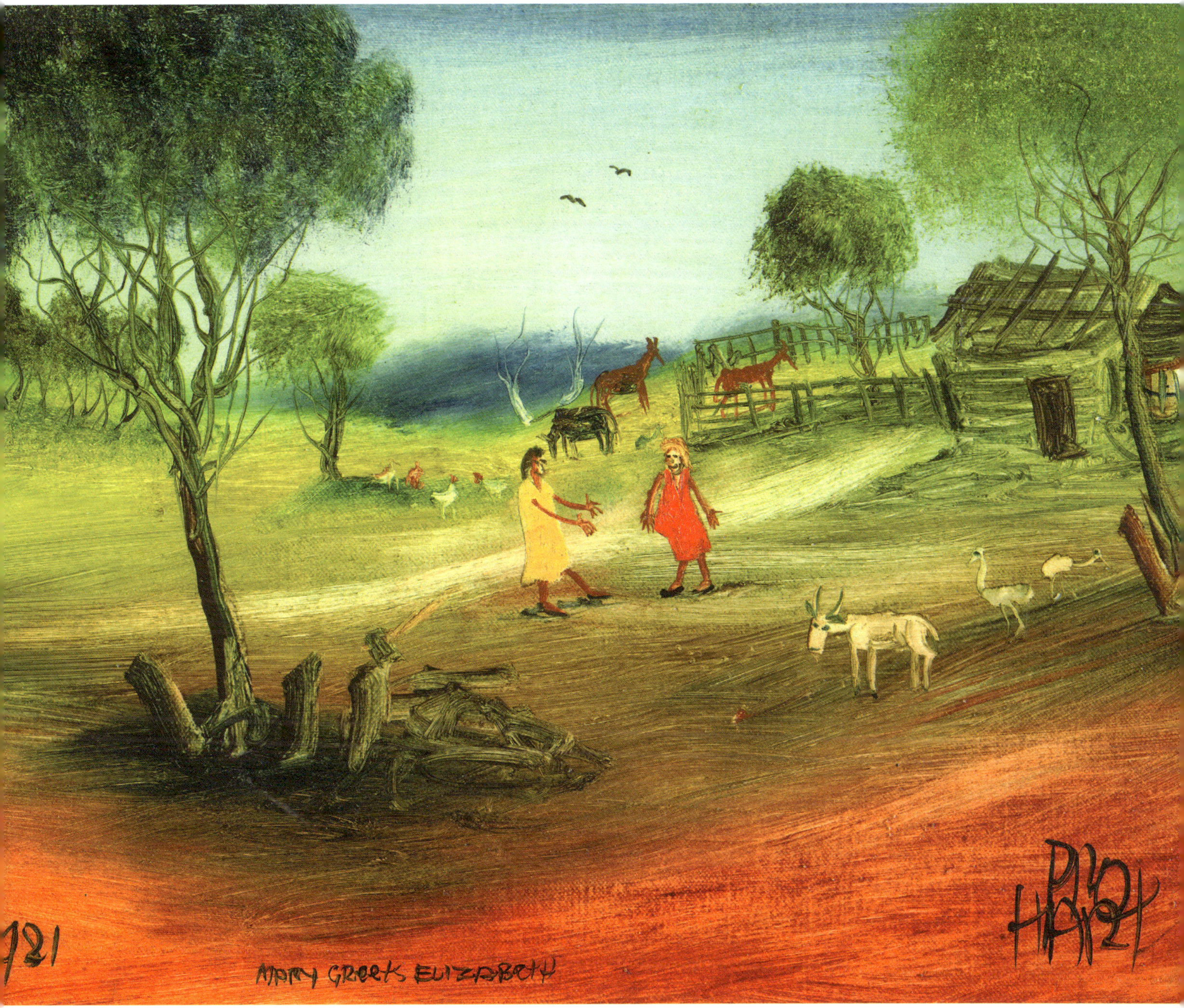
MARY GREETS ELIZABETH

Zechariah's Pride

God, it's good to be a father
and see your own son appear
as if you saw yourself
being born years before.
It's flamin' marvellous!

I got carried away when John was born
and I saw his scrawny little legs
kicking against the air
and jabbing his tender feet
blunt in his father's face.
Who did he think he was?
He was my kid, after all,
and I swear he looked like me.

'He ought to be called
the same as his dad.'
That's what the neighbours said.
'He sounds just like his father, anyway.'
They turned to me for reply,
but the words just would not come.
I could not find the word
to name my own son!
It was as if a great rock
was damming up my soul below
and crushing the gift of speech.

So I grabbed a scrap of paper
and scribbled, 'John'.
Name him John, I wrote,
just as the Outback angel said.
My friends all watched in silence
until the dam within me burst
and words like water
splashed on everyone in sight.

I preached and preached about my son.
That boy, I said, will blaze the promised track
for us to follow through the wilderness
and back to God.
I got carried away when John was born
but you have to be proud
of your wife and your son
at moments like this.

A chorus of crows out in the yard
echoed my inner pride,
'God, it's good to be a father!
Yes! It's great to have a son!'

Luke 1:57–80

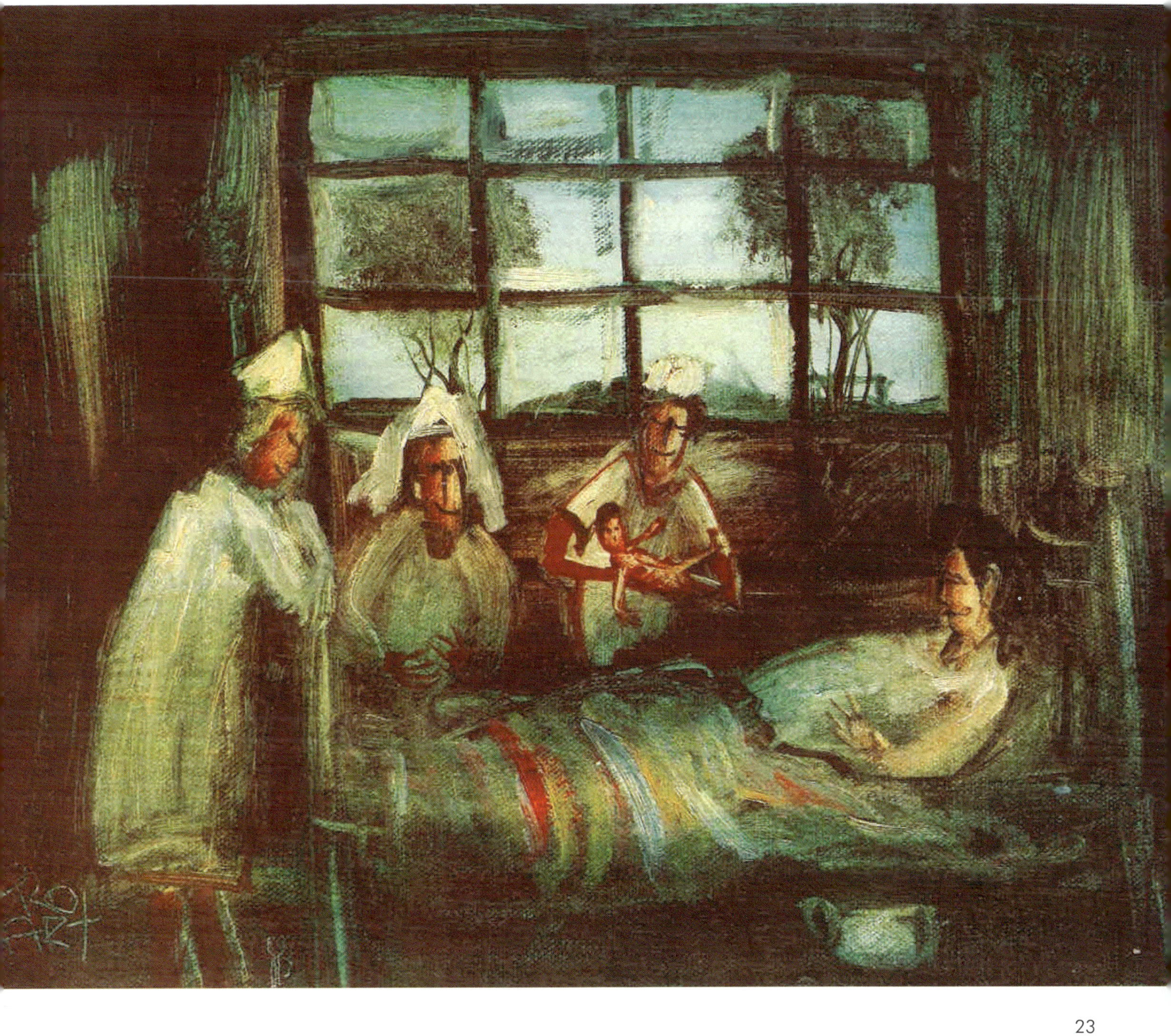

The Ride to Bethlehem

I have ridden hard with stockmen
on high mountain ranges
and worked long with drovers
on harsh runs out back,
I have crossed flooded rivers
with heavy bullock drays
and known lonely trips
with a swag upon my back,
but the ride down to Bethlehem
in a wild uncanny way
was rougher than a crossing
of the worst desert waste.

The governor had sent out word
that small folk like us
should go down to Bethlehem
to register their claims.
So down we rode, as honest folk,
down through the Outback scrub,
slowly, slowly winding
through the simmering Outback heat.

For miles they watched us travel
and wondered at our pace,
the dingoes and the lizards watched
from their hot rock lookouts overhead.
They watched, the nosey bandicoots,
the sulphur-crested cockatoos,
they watched a slender pregnant girl
ride slowly through the sun.

They watched, perhaps they wondered
how Mary's child would fare
if born among the long green ants
that riddle the burning scrub.
We rode and I too wondered
if God was watching now,
and waiting for his Son
to survive this burning bush.

For miles we rode on slowly
as heat waves flowed before us
and the pains began to stab
the hidden core of Mary's soul.
Then far beyond the last mirage
we saw a small bush town ahead,
a little town called Bethlehem
inviting us to rest.

Luke 2:1–5

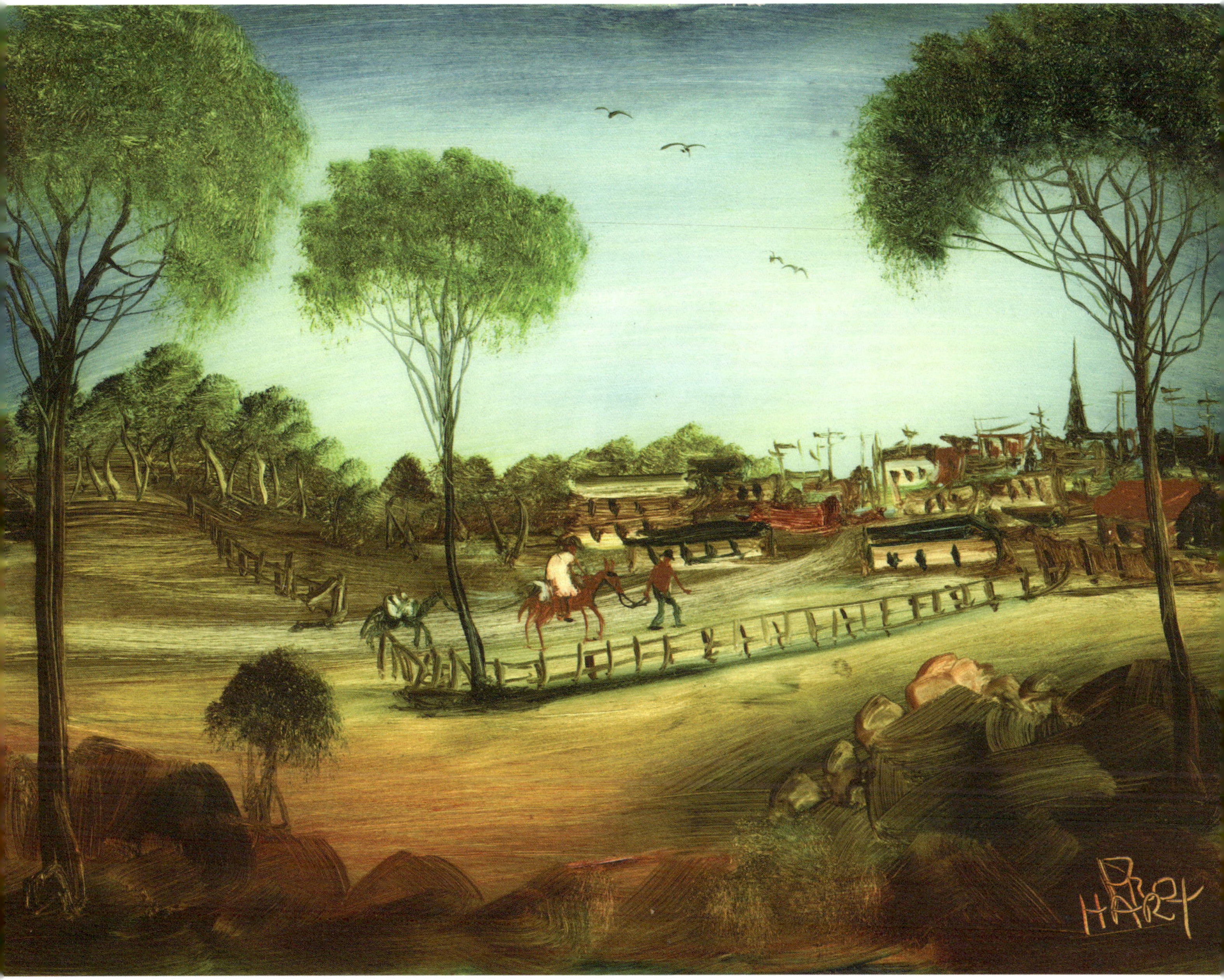

The Bethlehem Pub

A country pub is not a proper place for women,
the last place on earth to try and have a kid.
So when Mary and her tired old man arrived that night
I rustled up a bed of straw out in the shed.

I run the country pub in Outback Bethlehem,
a home away from home for stockmen interstate.
For when the picnic races stir the dust out here
a man will ride a hundred miles to meet his mate.

The pub in Bethlehem is rough as horned-head toads
and what I've seen would turn a shearer green and white,
like the time young Bill fought Blue, the old man kangaroo,
till beer and blood and fur flowed down the street.

I've seen men drive their horse in for a drink or two
and with their stockwhip clear the beer glass of its foam
while Fred, the pet galah, whose language turned the air dark blue,
would screech his old refrain, 'Well stone the flamin' crows'.

You should have heard the cursing from the stockmen when I said,
'We have a pregnant woman with the horses in the stalls.'
You should have seen them drinking, mate, and heard them sing off key:
'Why was he born so beautiful, why was he born at all?'

At first I also wondered if Mary's child belonged out here;
he may as well be born among the mulga bush out back.
Yet Mary seemed a sister to all who found her in the shed
and Jesus seemed a brother to drinkers, drovers, blacks.

Luke 2:7

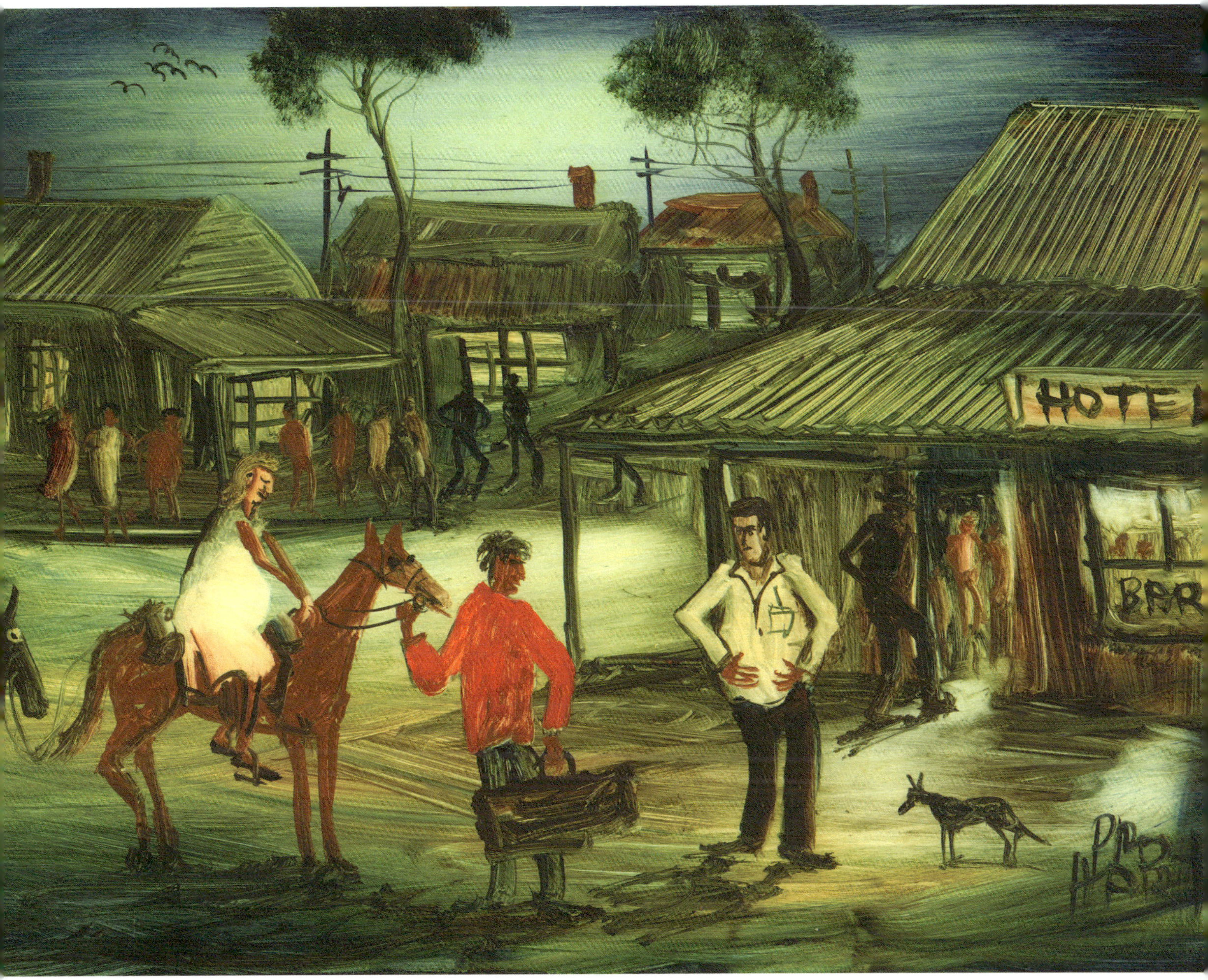
HOTE
BAR

Jesus' Birth

After the long anxious ride
through the smothering heat
to Bethlehem;
after the long loud night
of shouting stockmen in the pub,
of brave old drinkers hanging on,
of shearers telling wild tales,
of endless bawdy bush songs;
after the last slow dingo howl,
the last call of a hopeful bird,
the last long vicious pain
that broke my body open,
the night was silent.

In the silence of dawn
Jesus burst from my body,
gasping for life
and shedding his robe of blood.
Joseph grasped the warm child,
cut the pulsing cord
that still bound me to my son
and wiped the blood from his face.
We wrapped strips of torn cloth
around his soft shivering body
and laid him in a feed box
where the horses eat their hay.

In those few moments
Jesus felt the first plunge
of air into his timid chest,
the first splash of light
into his womb-blind eyes,
the first brush of rough male hands
against his quivering flesh,
the first odour into his lungs
of horses, straw, and last night's beer,
the first open space
of a wide threatening world
outside his mother's body.

The Silence was broken,
my son had been born
and God was a parent
. . . at last.

Luke 2:6

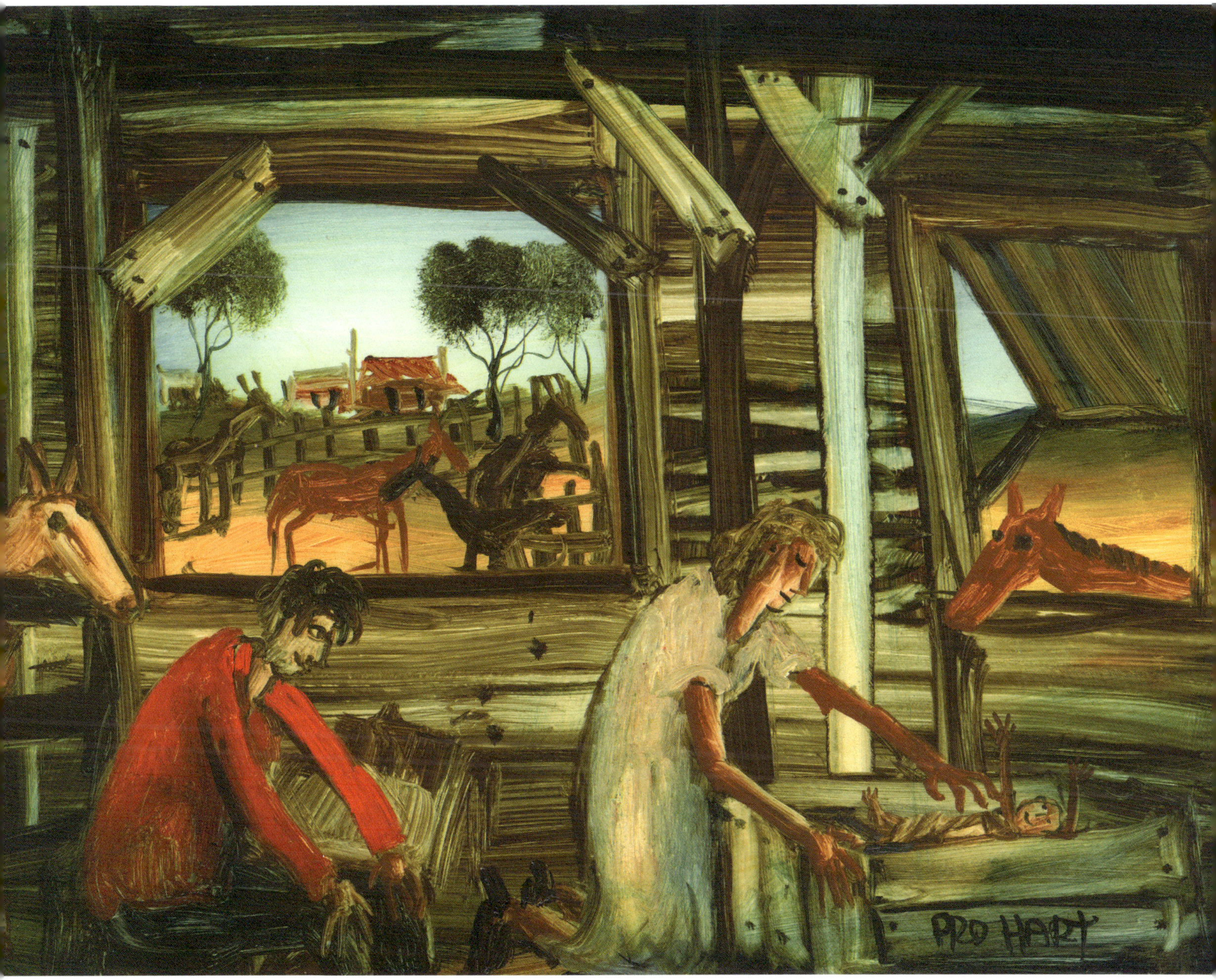
PRO HART

The Stockmen's Story

When stockmen like us
stare late into the fire at night
and poke the smoking mallet roots
we know no fear of dark.
We tell our tales of courage
crossing floods, defying storms,
and fighting fires in the bush
until our eyes are blind with smoke.
We know no fear of man or beast,
bushranger or ghost.

Yet the night the angels hit the camp
they scared us half to death.

A stranger wandered through the trees
from deep within the scrub.
'Round him hovered orange light,
the light we see when bushfire smoke
smothers out the sun
and turns the brown land orange grey.

'I have a message', said the stranger,
'about a baby born tonight.
You'll find the child wrapped up in rags
and lying in a feedbox
in a stable back of town.
This Outback boy, my friends,
is born to be your king,
a bushman sent from God.'

A frenzy filled the sky,
like a bush fire roaring overhead,
as flames of angels spat through space
and sang their blazing song
of glory to God on high
and peace to folk on earth.

None of us has been the same
since the angels hit the camp that night
and put the fear of God in us.

Luke 2:8–14

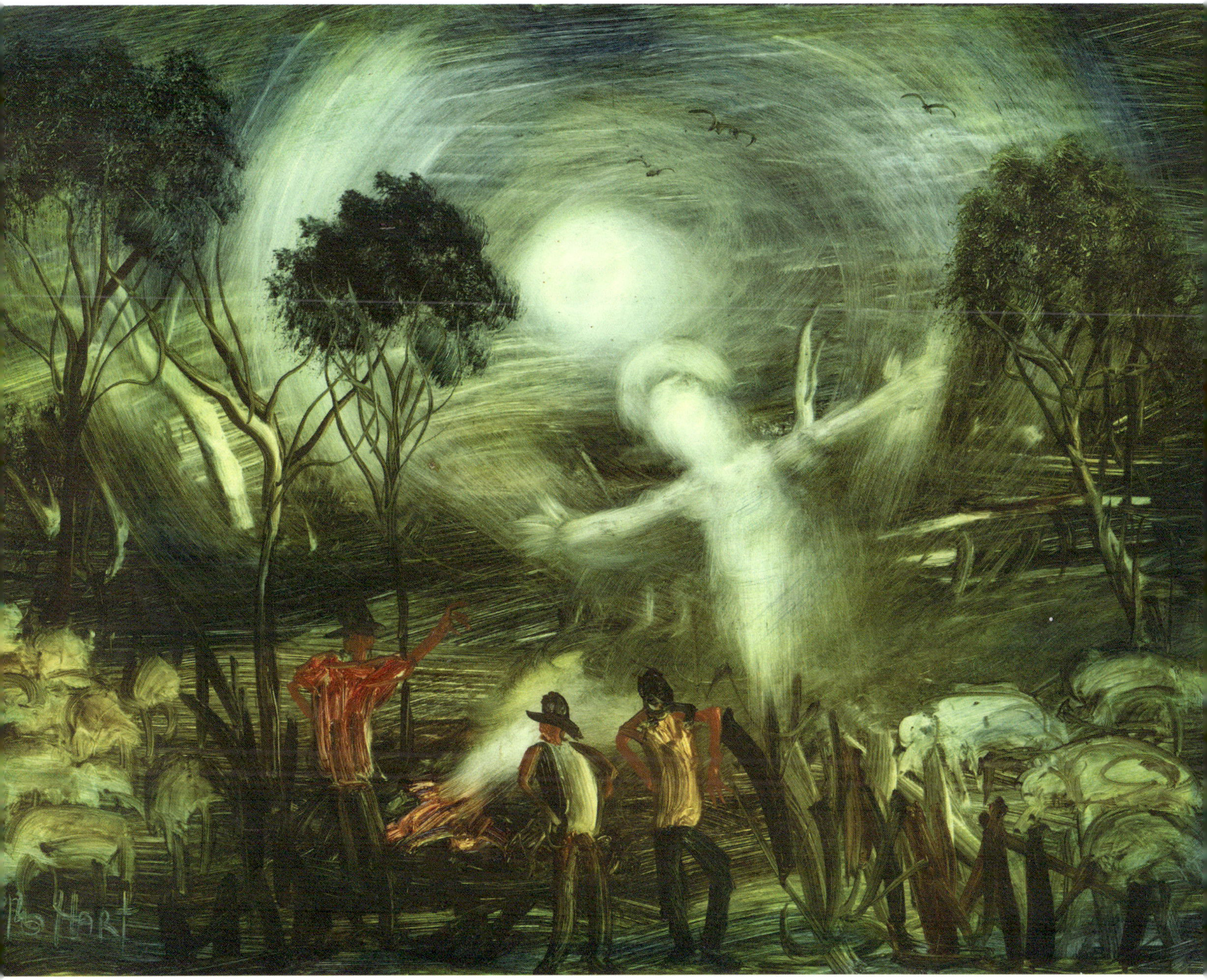
Pro Hart

Report of the Stockman

We found the baby Jesus
wrapped in strips of rag
and lying in a feedbox
in a shed.

His hands were red,
newborn red.

We heard the baby Jesus
lying in the straw
and crying for its mother
in the shed.

His face was red,
newborn red.

We believe the baby Jesus
dreaming in the hay
was God who came to find us
in a shed.

His flesh was red,
newborn red.

Like ours,
his hands, his face, his flesh
were red.

So we told the world
that God is one of us,
red flesh,
red face
and all.

Luke 2:15–20

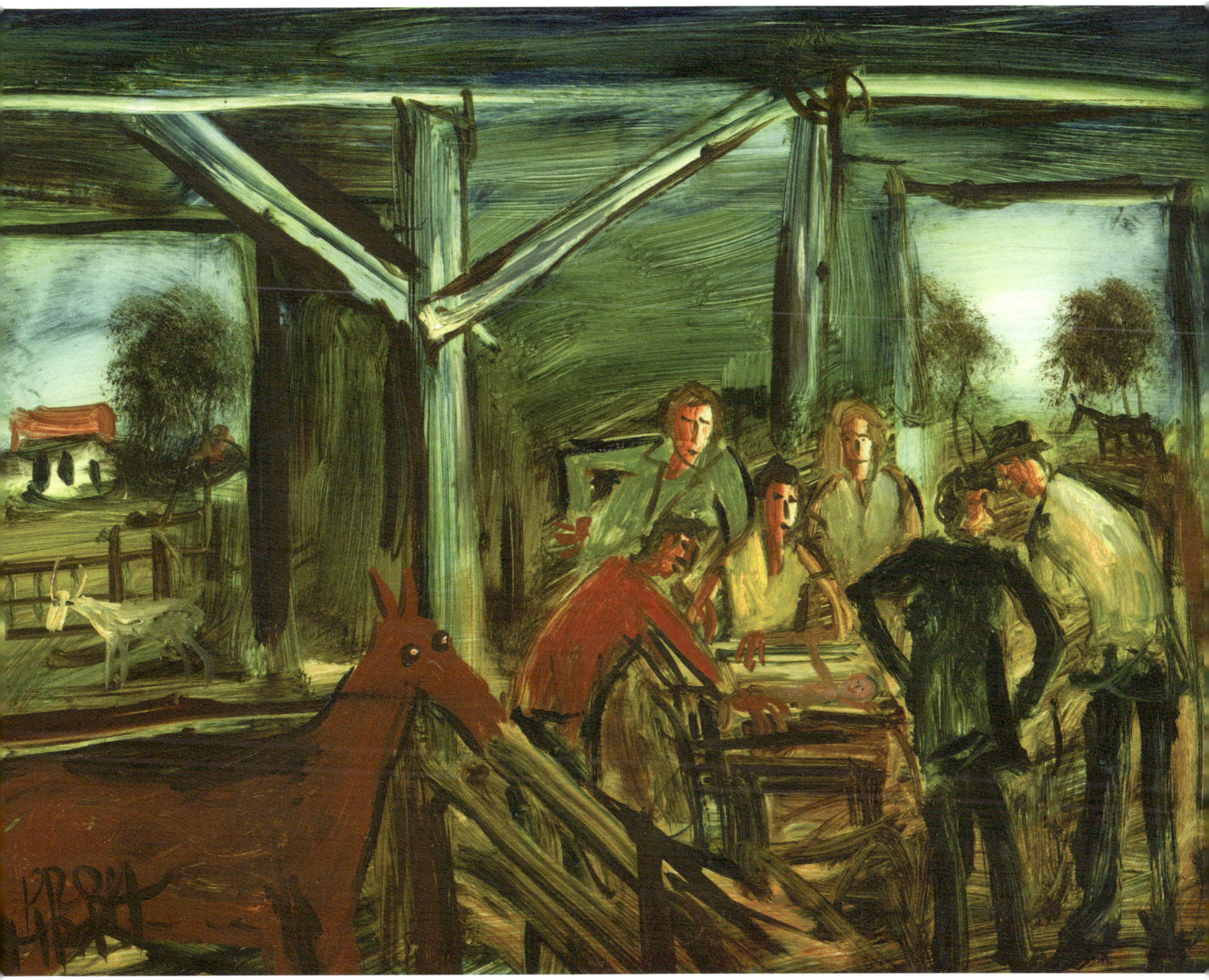

Mary's Gift

For long months I pondered
my child within me,
the line of its nose,
the turn of its face.
I wondered in pain
if the lurking shadow of God
had shaped form
or deformity within my womb.

Then we were two,
Jesus and I,
facing each other
with shocks of wonder,
touching each other's eyes
with lingering questions.

He lay in my open palms,
so small,
oh so small,
as if the pressure of my fingers
would count as cruelty.

There in the earth of my hands
I saw life itself,
life like silent breath
emerging from the sands of death,
life like a stark red flower
crying amid the white limestone fields,
life like a single blue wren
skating across black granite boulders,
life so precious
the pain of holding it was unbearable.

In that child I saw
the flesh of every child,
warm flesh that bleeds,
enfolds, and quivers at the hope
of being man or woman,
yet true to that same flesh
as sun and wind and Outback dust
toughen skin and soul alike.

This child was my flesh,
my flower, my son,
mine.
I was ready to defy God
and make that child mine,
forever mine
against all thieves
who sought to possess him.

Later, in the house of God,
I gave my child back to God
and with my flesh I gave
two birds to celebrate the day,
two birds to fly,
two birds to die
and redeem my child for life.

Luke 2:22–24

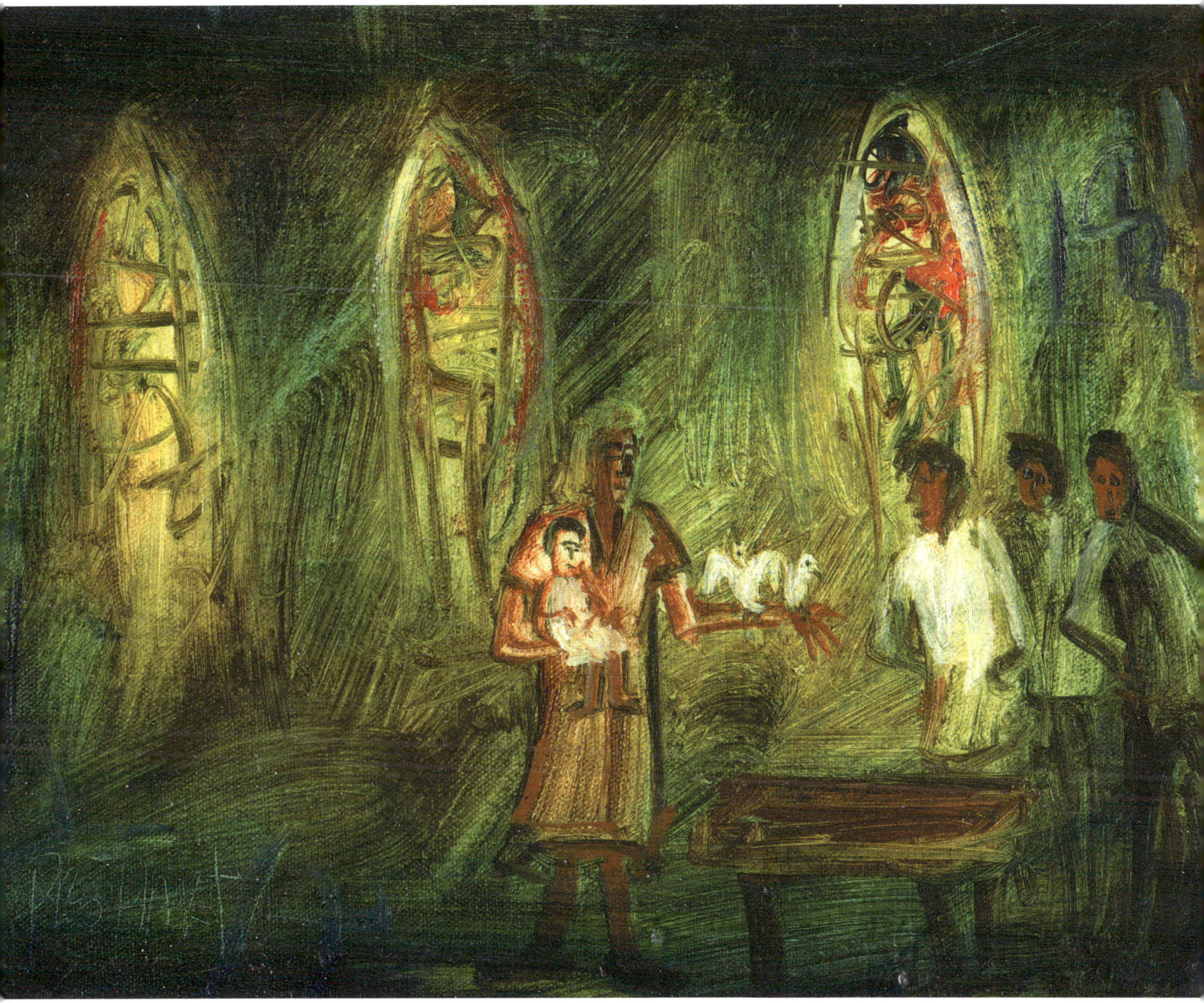

Simeon's Farewell

Being a prophet is rough
and bloody lonely at times.
A prophet has no mates.
only a hard-headed desert God
who sends us out as hunters
forever on unfriendly roads
with nothing but worries,
God's worries in our sack.

We are called to shock people
into seeing the cold truth,
the ugly selfish ways they live,
knocking others to boost themselves,
grabbing power by crushing hopes,
and hunting blacks as vermin.
God says some people are bastards,
stuck-up heartless bastards.
And we get no thanks
telling people truths like that . . .
only more flamin' worries.

I had a wild bush fantasy once
that I would see an Outback Christ
come riding into town as king.
Then I would leave to die in peace
bequeathing all my worries to him.
How I longed for that great hour.

When Mary brought young Jesus
into God's house for a blessing,
I knew this was the Outback Boy,
the promised king of the bush
who would take my swag of burdens.
I could see myself fly back to God,
deep in a wilderness gorge
where brolgas dance in desert shade
to welcome souls for death.

So with the Baby Jesus before me
I exploded with one more oracle:

Now let me die in peace, Lord,
and go to the great Never Never,
for this is the kid God promised,
the Bushman sent from the Silence
to be our Outback Saviour.
No worries now, Lord.
No worries, ever!

Luke 2:25–35

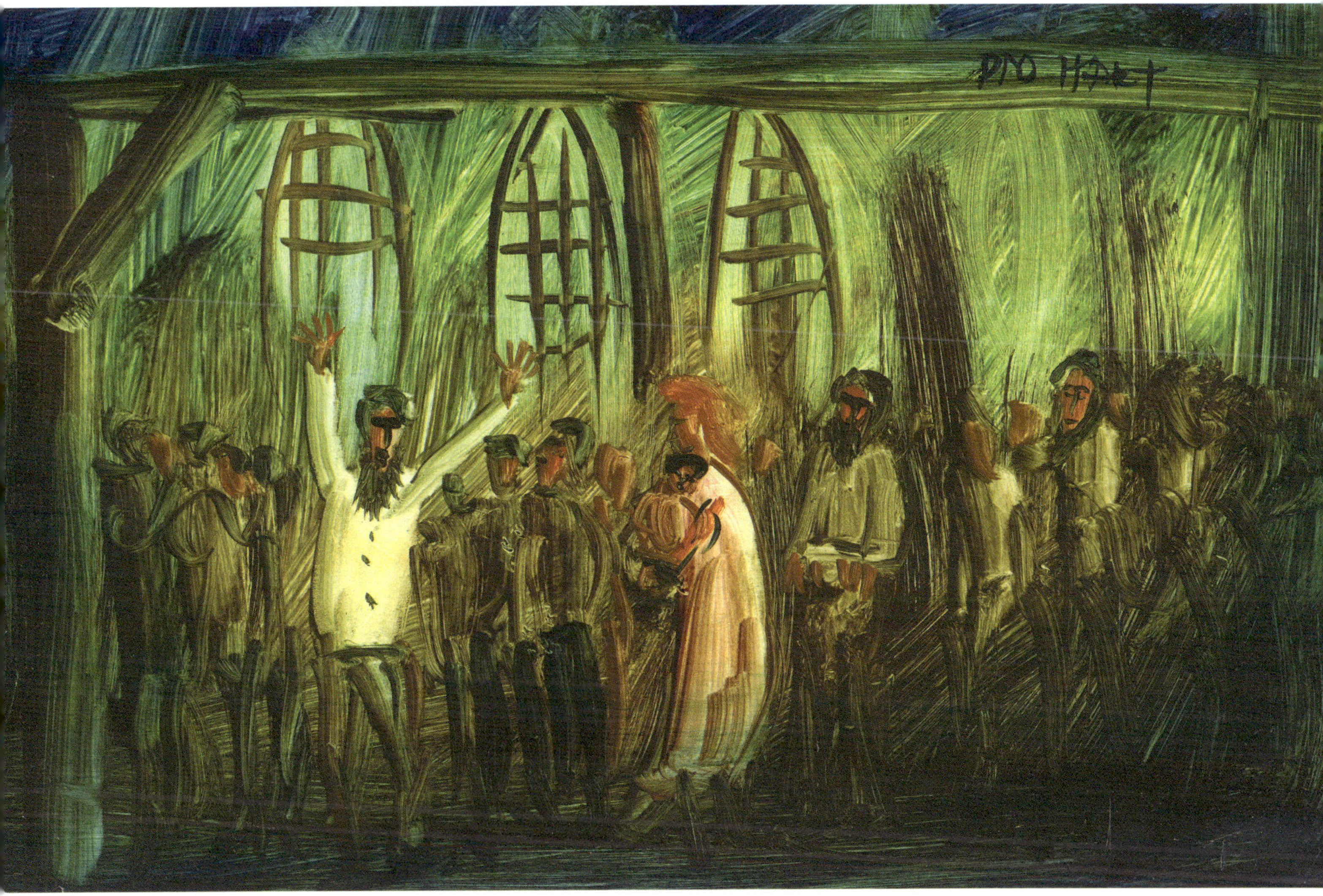

Anna's Song

I am a very old woman.
I have been old
almost as long as I can remember,
old like the grey rocks
grinning with wisdom on the hillside
where they wait and wait.

The day Mary came to worship
with Jesus her child,
I could wait no longer.
I was young again.
I had an urge to let go, wild
like a child fresh out of school
chasing her dream down the road
to nowhere.

When I saw the babe Jesus
I just adored him
and the words of my song
fell everywhere
like rain on the dry dust:

Lift this child to the sun,
Raise this child to the sky,
God has come from above,
Come to earth from on high.

Lay this child on the ground,
One with us, one with earth;
Let God know in his Son
Human clay, human birth.

Place this child in the shade,
Hang this child 'neath a tree;
With his hand on the wood
May this child set us free.

Give this child to the world,
Let him be common folk;
God has come to be born
As an ordin'ry bloke.

Send this child down the road,
Let him ride hard the track;
To be king of the bush
And the harsh world out back.

Lift this child to the night,
To the Silence of God;
Let this child cry for us
And the Silence be heard.

Luke 2:36–38

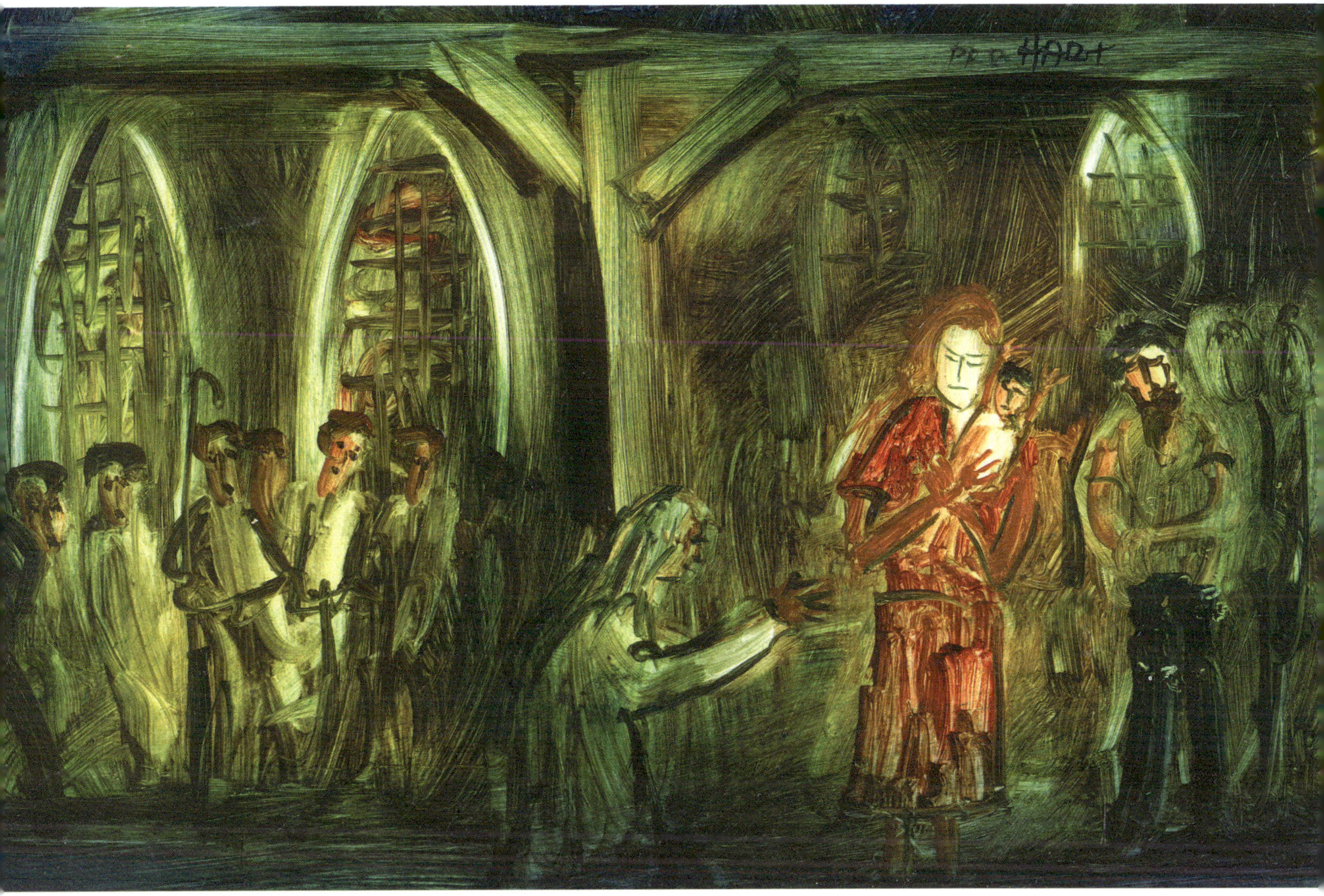

The Three Gamblers

We were fools,
wise old fools sailing out at night
into the treacherous wilderness
like the dazed explorers before us.
The shadows of death were watching,
the biting sun, the scorching ants,
the wild devil dog,
the wide dry waterholes,
the saltbush wastes and the bones.

The bones
like shining markers
reflecting the light of the star ahead
exposed the white bone road
to hollow dreams.

Was the star a trick,
a twist of light
turning our minds to follow
like the tip of some diviner's rod?
Was it a midnight mirage,
a blind man's hallucination,
a brilliant bird?
We never knew.

Yet we took the chance as gamblers must,
as explorers must,
as drovers must.
We took the bet
that this new star was a sign,
a silver omen of all our dreams out back.
We craved a leader,
a champion for the bush,
the battler foretold
by wise drovers long ago.

We left our mates unrolling their swags
beside a beckoning fire.
'Bet you never make it alive',
the lead drover yelled.
'Bet you ten beers we do',
we each in turn replied.

With the smell of cold ale in our teeth
we rode into the dry desert night
following our star
our bold stroke of hope
and luck.

Matthew 2:1–2

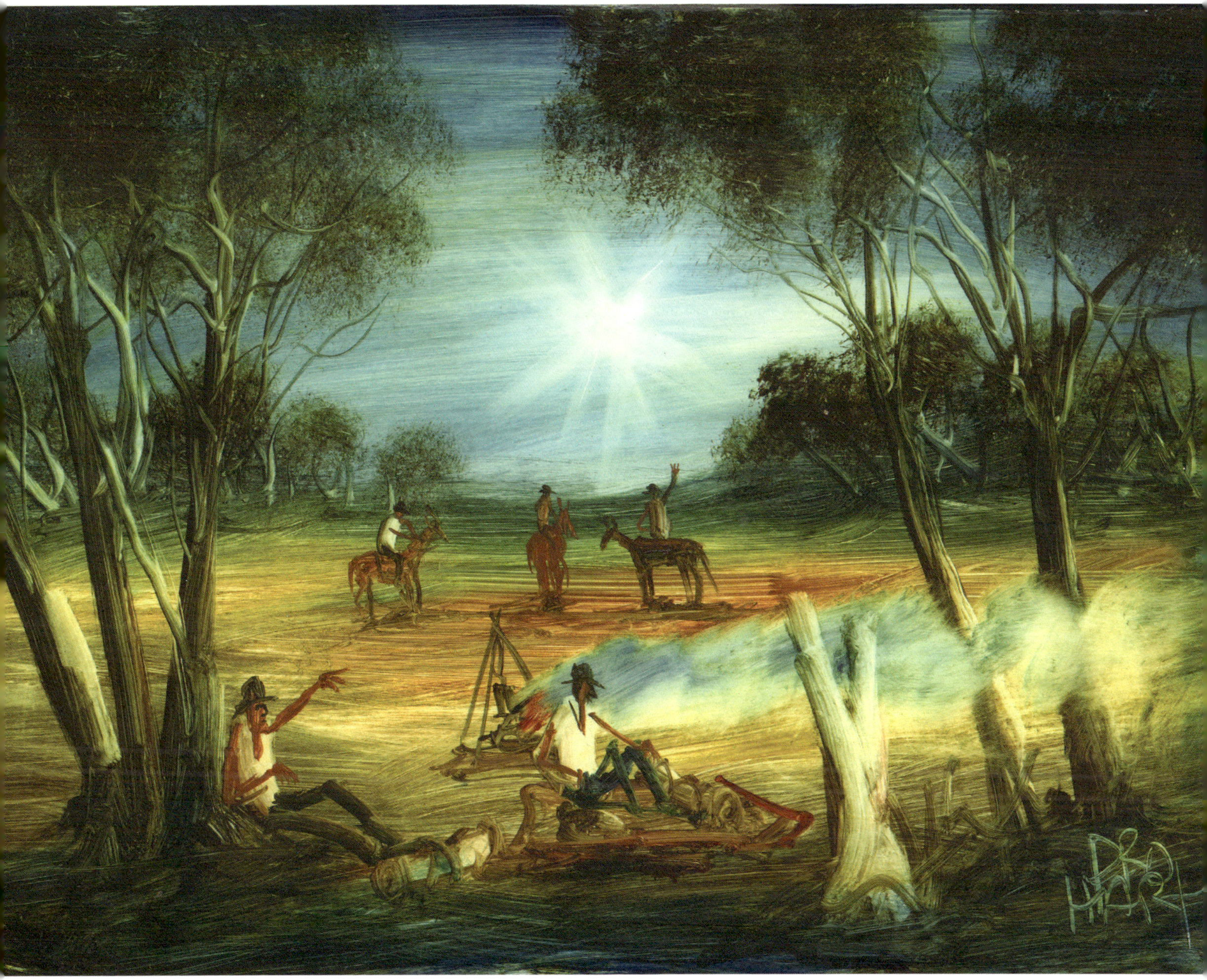

Gold Rush

As we rode into the night
the star travelled before us
on a sky road overhead,
like a wild celestial horseman
bent for the great Never Never.

Stockmen, drovers, farmers,
trackers, outlaws,
gamblers all,
flung out barbs of hope
as we passed down the road
to nowhere known.

'Where are you going, mate?
Out West, back of hell?'

'What are you chasing, mate?
A horse in the flamin' sky?'

'What if you catch him, mate?
Will you ride him in the Cup?'

'What's at the end of it, mate?
A kangaroo to ride back home?'

'Have you lost something, mate?
Or is there gold out back?'

Gold!
The word fell like fire
igniting afresh
lost dreams of tired men and women,
gamblers all,
ready to have their worlds
for the call of gold! gold! gold!

We rode together into the black,
the endless moaning black
chasing our star,
our gold,
our horseman of the Never Never.

Little did we dream
the star would lead a path
to an unknown country boy
as poor as any child
lost in the mallee scrub.

Matthew 2:1

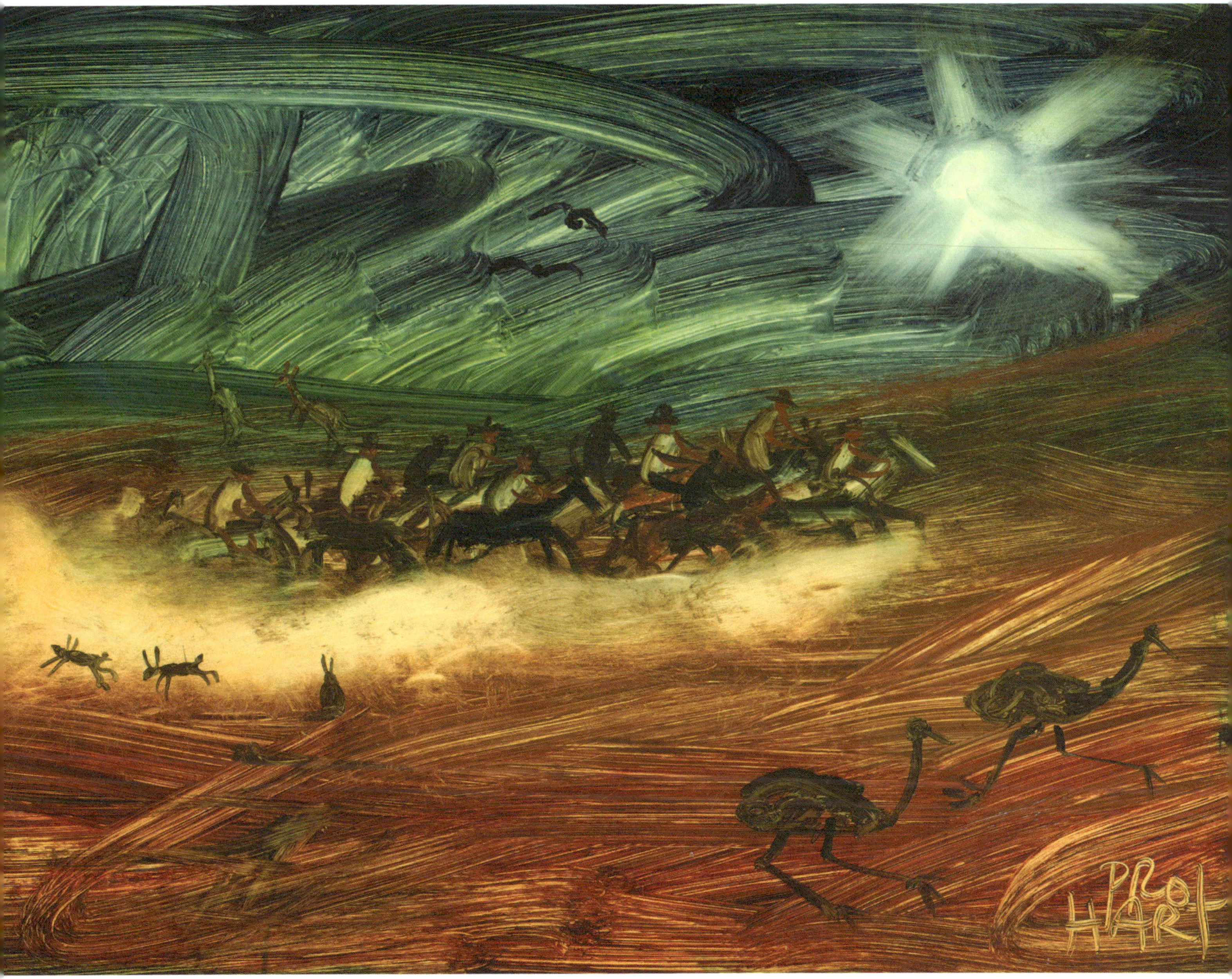
PRO HART

Herod's Apology

They were only a mob of stirrers,
deluded drovers from way out back.
They came in breathing dust and sweat
from riding hard through sun-baked sands
and following a sleepless star,
or so they tried to say.
They were searching for some local kid
to be their drover king,
the latest thing in petty Outback politics.

I had to humour them.

I called a special meeting
of the ranking religious in town
to cheek the size of the dream.
They believed a king would be born
in a small bush town called Bethlehem.
Bethlehem—absurd!—Bethlehem,
where the goats outnumber the people
and the gossips outdo the goats.

I had to humour them.

I poured a glass of the best red
to wet the baby's head
and another glass for the road.
I told them to keep me informed
of the state of play in Bethlehem
so I could do the right thing
and pay my respects to the boy,
which I fully intended to do.

But the rotters never returned
and something had to be done.
We cannot have strangers trooping through town
in search of a kid with a crown
and stirring a shearer's revolt.
Someone has to keep order
in this God-forsaken plot of land.
So I sent my men
to pick up any suspicious babies
in the outlying country towns
and crush this talk of a king
before it turned to treason.

I mean, something had to be done,
someone had to make a decision.
So I killed the little brats!

Matthew 2:3–8

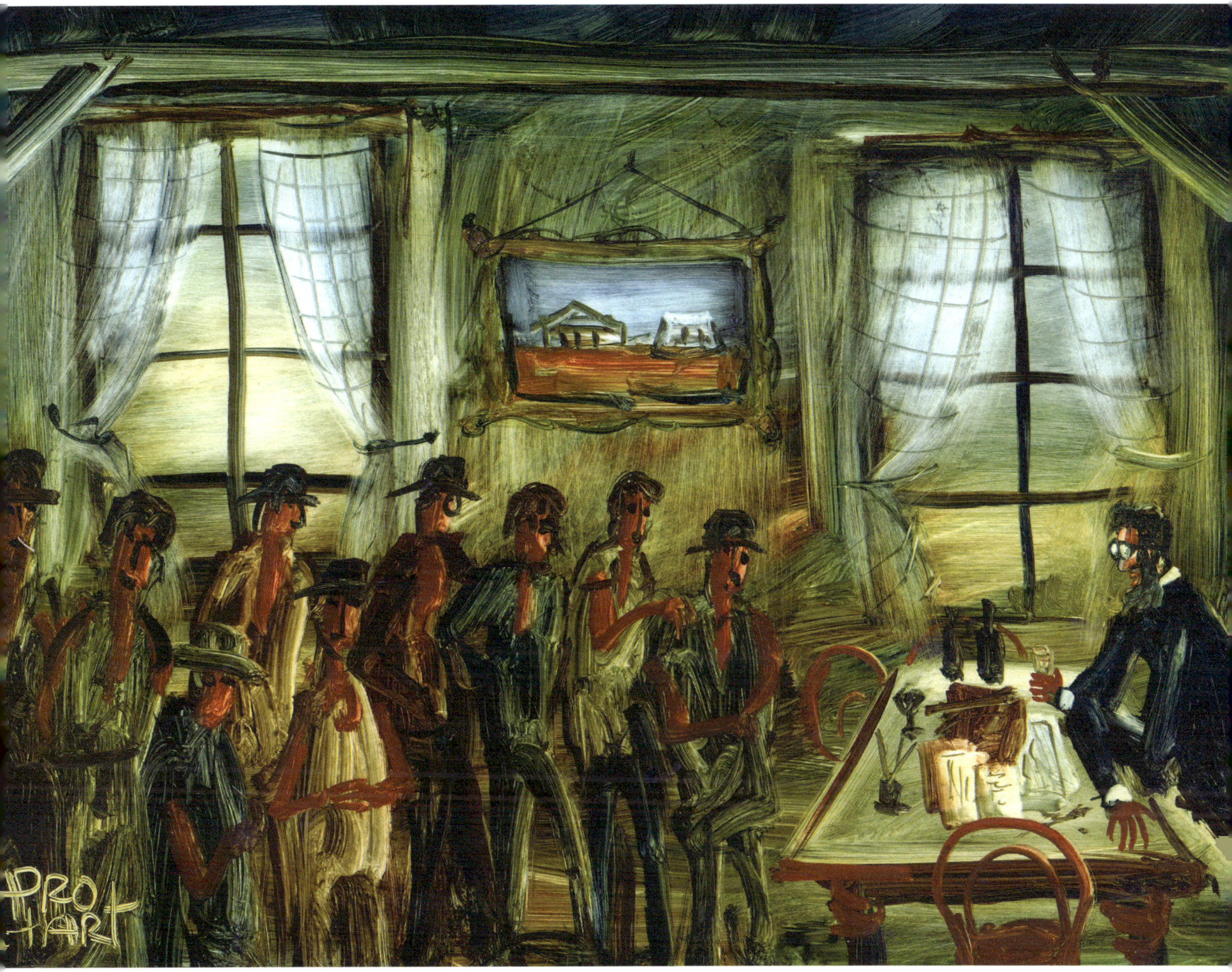
PRO
HART

The Gifts of the Gamblers

There he was,
the kid, the king!
Yes, there he was,
a clumsy, crinkly faced Christ
kicking his tiny feet in the air
and poking his fingers
into his mother's face.

What do you say to a kid from God?
'Your tiny highness,
welcome to the bush.
Glad you could join us.
Hope you had a good trip.'

What do you give to a kid from God?
'Here is an old nugget
my father kept from the gold-rush days.
It looks a bit green
but she's pure gold inside.
Perhaps you could make a crown.'

'Here is a drop of vintage port
I collected on the Southern run
and kept for a special day.
It'll keep till you're twenty-one.'

'This here is the hide of a wallaby
I tanned meself last winter.
It smells a bit like tanning bark
but it'll keep the insects away.'

'This is a stone with secret signs,
for we who are blacks here know
that you have the spirit of the crying tree
from the dreaming tracks you crossed.'

The wise visitors
celebrated their luck.
Mary said thanks.
And the baby Jesus . . .
wept!

Matthew 2:9–12

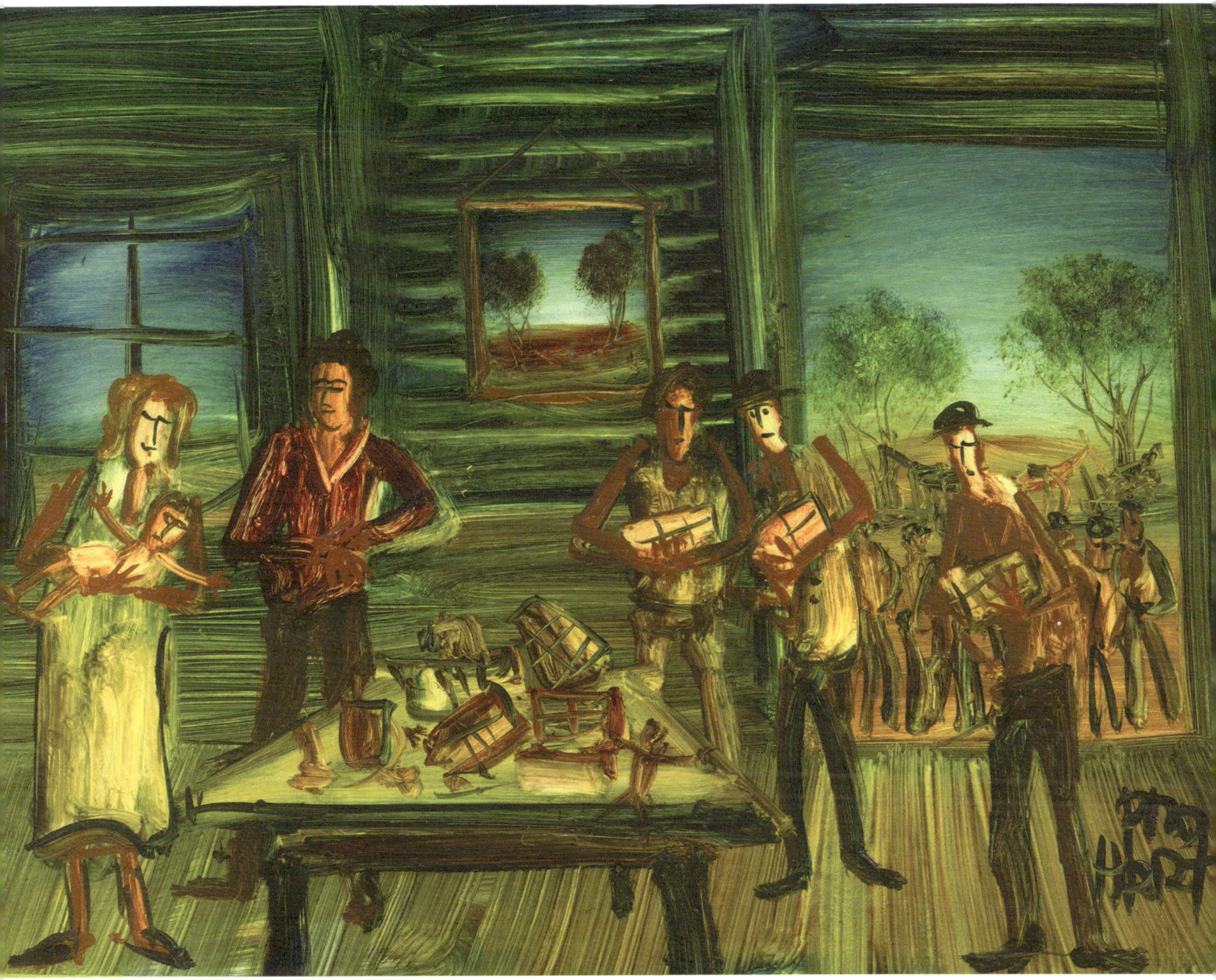

The Flight

By night the warning came to flee
as with each baby's cry
King Herod sent out messengers
inviting us to die.

We fled into the wilderness
like plunging through the eye
of life's vast unseen enemy
inviting us to die.

Eternal rocks rose stark and red
against the white hot sky,
eternal chasms rose like graves
inviting us to die.

Cross endless plains of burning earth
where only fierce ants fly,
sharp tongues of grass like barbed wire
invited us to die.

The empty saltbeds, soaks, and streams
were filled with nought but dry
and from their pulsing souls beneath
invited us to die.

The god of this great barren earth
blew sand into the sky
and spun a waterless mirage
inviting us to die.

We journeyed through the land of death
beyond where dead men lie
and brought this hidden child back home
as life for all who die.

Matthew 2:13–15

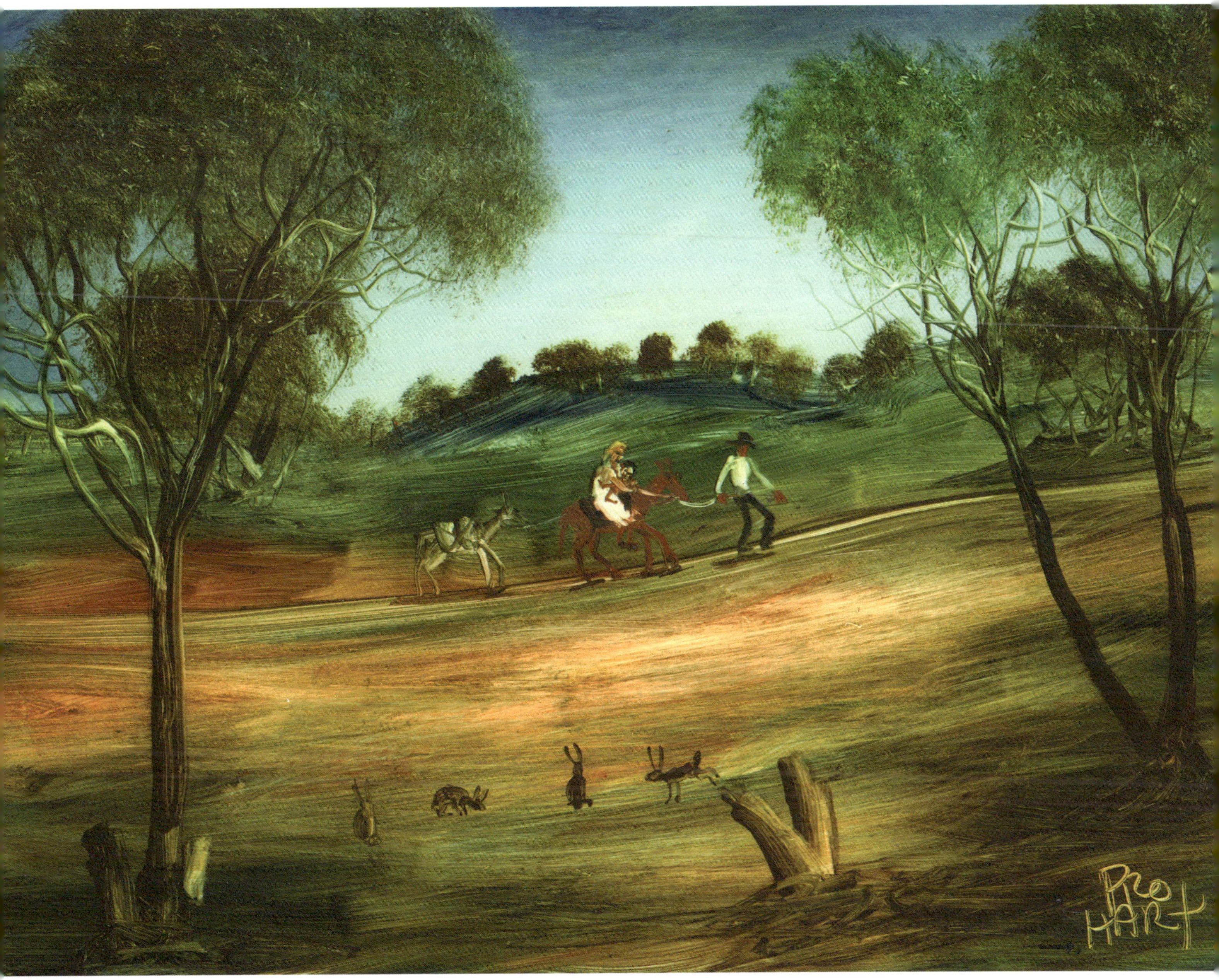
PRO HART

Coming Home

After our long flight through death,
our journey through wide bitter wastes,
we came home to Nazareth,
home to our small town,
our family.
As we shuffled along
the wattles whispered a song to our son
and white-winged birds scattered
greetings across the waking landscape.
Their joy heralded afar
the song of future families
following the steps of our child
back home:

Will you be coming home this Christmas
Before this lonely year is done?
Will you be born a child among us
To make our family one?

Will you be driving through the desert
Across the wastes where dingoes roam?
Will you return our drover brother
To heal our broken home?

Will you be coming home a swagman,
Your billy slung across your back,
And set our weary feet in rhythm
Along the homeward track?

Will you return a lost explorer
And wander in with broken breath
To celebrate a new tomorrow
Without the fear of death?

Will you be coming home with Mary,
Brown girl with child upon her knee?
Will you be home to reunite us
Beneath a Christmas tree?

Will you be coming from the Centre
A traveller sent from God Outback,
To stir the goodness deep among us
As we follow down the track.

Will you be coming home this Christmas
Before this lonely year is done?
Will you be coming from the Outback
To make our family one?

Matthew 2:39

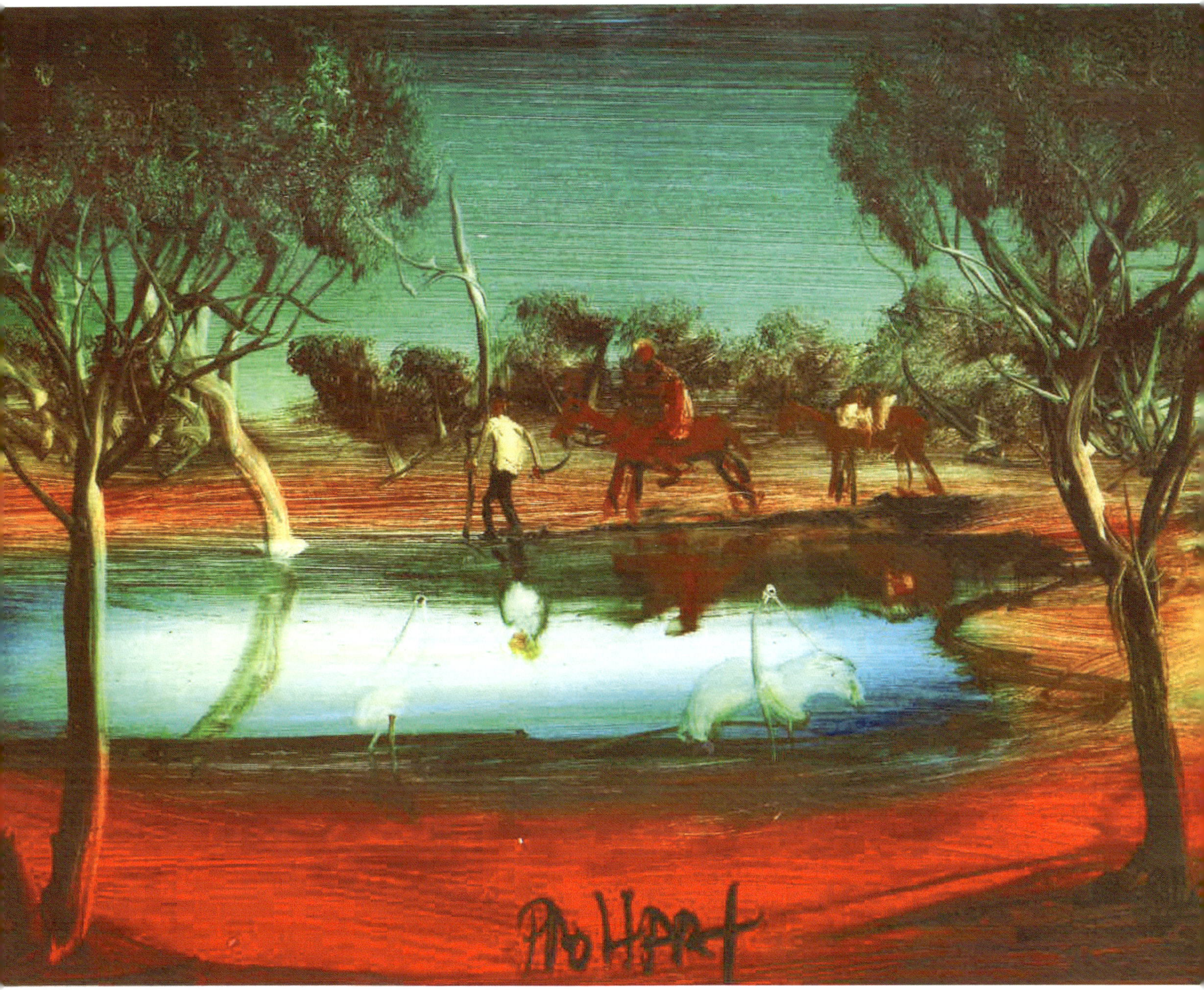
Pro Hart

About the Author

NORMAN HABEL

Norman Habel is currently Professorial Fellow at Flinders University. He has long been involved in issues of biblical interpretation and social justice. His research includes The Earth Bible, a five volume international project with other scholars reading the Bible from the perspective of justice for Earth. A sequel to these volumes is the Earth Bible Commentary series which was launched in 2011, the first volume of which is his work entitled: The Birth, the Curse and the Greening of Earth. His latest publications are entitled Exploring Ecological Hermeneutics, An Inconvenient Text and A Rainbow of Mysteries.

He is a long term student of the Old Testament Book of Job, having written the commentary on Job

About the Illustrator

Pro Hart

Pro Hart (Kevin Charles Hart) was born in 1928 in the New South Wales town of Broken Hill, and spent his early years on a family owned sheep station. A world renowned artist who had for many years an art gallery in Broken Hill and is widely regarded as the father of Australian Outback painting and admired for capturing the spirit of the Outback. In his later life he developed motor Neurone disease and was unable to paint for the last six months of his life and died in 2006. He was made an a Member of the Order of the British Empire in 1976.

Outback Christmas is a significant book, first published in 1981, and is now released with a new Preface. This new edition is released ten years after the death of the artist, Pro Hart. Most of our Christmas art and verse have been inherited from English and European sources, but the Christian message is universal and other cultures commonly portray the characters and events surrounding Christ's birth in line with local custom. This book portrays the nativity of Christ in bold images of the Australian Outback.

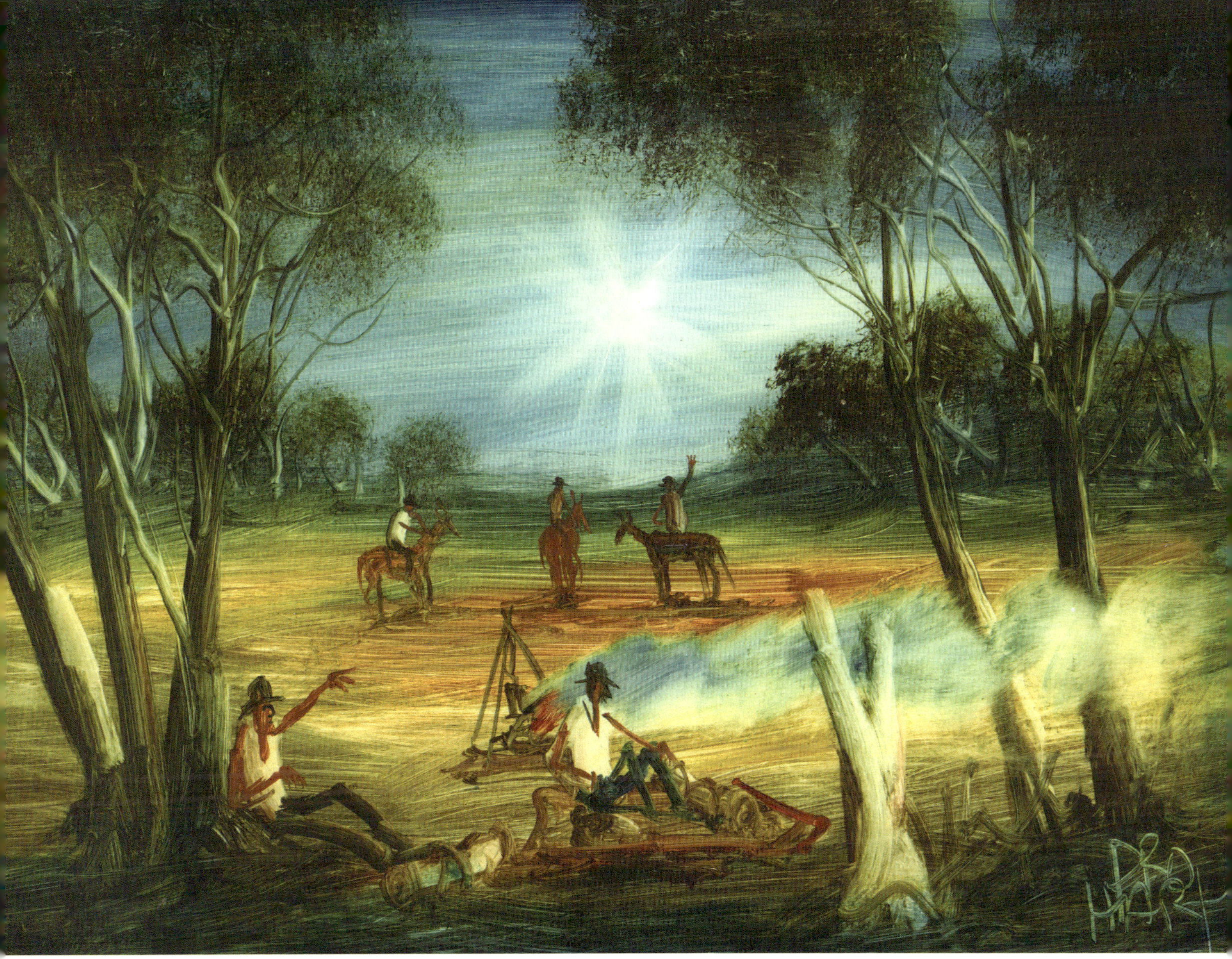

CPSIA information can be obtained at www.ICGtesting.com
Printed in the USA
BVIW12n1941230217
476808BV00001B/1
* 9 7 8 1 9 2 5 3 0 9 4 9 2 *